Ama

Everything You Should Know About Amazon Echo Dot From Beginner To Advanced

Table of Contents

INTRODUCTION 6

CHAPTER 1: AMAZON ECHO DOT – THE EVOLUTION BEGINS 8
    THE REASON FOR THE SEASON 8
    GOOD MORNING ALEXA 9
    ALEXA'S SKILLS 11
    ULTIMATE GOAL: THE SMART HOME 12
    THE PROBLEM WITH ACCENTS 13
    THE GOOD AND THE BAD 13

CHAPTER 2: HELLO ALEXA 14
    ALEXA ORIGINS 14
    THE WORLD OF VIRTUAL ASSISTANTS 15
    AVAILABLE FUNCTIONS 16
    CRITIQUES AND AUDIENCE RECEPTION 18

CHAPTER 3: GETTING STARTED WITH THE AMAZON ECHO DOT 19
    BUTTONS AND PARTS 19
    DIFFERENCES BETWEEN 1ST AND 2ND GENERATION MODELS 23
    ECHO DOT SETUP 23
    CONNECTING TO EXTERNAL SPEAKERS 28
    CONNECTING YOUR ECHO DOT TO EXTERNAL SPEAKERS USING AN AUDIO CABLE 30

CHAPTER 4: USING THE ALEXA REMOTE 31
    PAIR THE ALEXA VOICE REMOTE WITH YOUR ECHO DOT 32

CHAPTER 5: CONNECTING YOUR ECHO DOT 33
    CONNECTING TO A WIFI HOTSPOT 34
    CONNECTING YOUR ECHO DOT TO WIRELESS NETWORK 35
    PAIRING WITH BLUETOOTH DEVICES 37

PAIRING WITH BLUETOOTH SPEAKERS 37
CONNECTING YOUR MOBILE DEVICE TO YOUR ECHO DOT 38
CONNECTING YOUR ALEXA VOICE REMOTE 39
CONTROLLING PAIRED DEVICES VIA VOICE 39
CONNECTING SPEAKERS VIA AUDIO CABLE 40
CONNECTING SMART DEVICES 41
CERTIFIED SPEAKER 41
BLUETOOTH PROFILES SUPPORTED BY ALEXA 41
COMPATIBLE BLUETOOTH SPEAKERS 42

CHAPTER 6: ALEXA'S OPERATIONAL BASICS 45

MODES OF ACTIVATION 45
SHE GETS SMARTER 46
REVIEWING YOUR INTERACTIONS WITH ALEXA 47
VOICE PURCHASING 48
WORKING WITH SMART DEVICES 49

CHAPTER 7: GETTING THINGS DONE WITH ALEXA .. 50

REMEMBER THE WAKE WORD 50
WHAT IF YOU WANT TO CHANGE THE WAKE WORD? 50
MOST BASIC COMMANDS AROUND THE HOUSE 51
ASKING ALEXA SOME INTERESTING QUESTIONS PLUS COMMANDS . 52
DATES AND TIME 52
A BIT OF MATH 52
STATISTICS AND FACTS 53
ALEXA IN THE KITCHEN 53
ALEXA AND CALENDARS 54
PLAYING AND MANAGING YOUR MUSIC 55
TIME, DATE, APPOINTMENTS AND SUCH 55
MUSIC AND MEDIA 56
USE YOUR ECHO DOT TO CONTROL YOUR FIRE TV OR FIRE TV
STICKS 58
MAKING A CALL AND COMMANDS FOR MESSAGING 59
BUYING STUFF 59
SHOPPING NOTIFICATIONS 60
SHOPPING LISTS AND TO DO LISTS 61
WEATHER REPORT AND FLASH BRIEFINGS 61
FOOD AND ENTERTAINMENT INFORMATION 62

3

Sports Stuff 63
Usual Commands for a Smart Home System 63
Voice Commands for User Accounts and Profiles 64

CHAPTER 8: ALEXA'S EASTER EGGS 65

Discovering the Easter Eggs 66
Other Movie References 68
Music References 69
Jokes and Candid Answers (Some of them can be a bit Off Tangent) 70

CHAPTER 9: ALEXA AND HER GROWING NUMBER OF SKILLS 71

What's a Skill Anyway? 71
Managing the Skills on Your Echo Dot 73
Amassing Support 75
Going Beyond the Out of the Box Experience 75
Skill Finder 76
Capital One Skill 77
Coinbase Bitcoin/Ethereum Price 79
Motley Fool Stock Watch 80
Reuters TV (World) 80
Daily Tech Headlines 81
Automatic Skill 81
Top Music Chart 82
Sleep and Relaxation Sounds 82
AnyPod 82

CHAPTER 10: WORKING WITH SMART HOME DEVICES 83

Preliminaries 83
Guidelines for Each Smart Device 84
Connecting Your Smart Home Device 85
How to Use Alexa to Operate Smart Devices 86
Making Alexa Work with Smart Home Cameras 88
No More Fidgeting Over Amazon Boxes on Your Front Door 88

How to Setup Alexa to Work with Home and Smart Cameras 90
How To Mount Your Cloud Cam 94
Connecting Smart Lights to Your Echo Dot 95

CHAPTER 11: SETTING UP AN ALEXA SMART HOME .96

Consider the Location 97
Setting Up Your Smart Devices 98
Getting Your Devices in Sync with Alexa 99
Setting Up Device Groups and Scenes 99
Take Time to Fine Tune Things 100
Connecting Your Echo Dot to IFTTT 101

CHAPTER 12: TROUBLESHOOTING COMMON PROBLEMS 102

Funky Light Ring 102
Can't Find Smart Home Devices/Appliances 103
Can't Connect to Current Smart Devices 103
Echo Dot Disconnects from WiFi 103
Echo Dot Can't Understand What You're Saying 104
Echo Dot Accidentally Gets Activated 104
Getting Unwanted Calls 104
Alarms are Too Loud 105
Problems Streaming Musing 105
Playing Music in the Wrong Speaker 105

CONCLUSION 106

5

Introduction

Welcome new Amazon Echo Dot owner. Well, this book assumes that you are a brand spanking new owner of the Amazon Echo Dot – the younger and much smaller version of the original Amazon Echo. Needless to say, this book is designed for the absolute beginner and first time Alexa user. In this book we'll go over every detail of this device so that you can know how it works inside and out. You will learn how to set it up and how to take advantage of its many features.

The Out of the Box Experience

Getting a new gizmo is absolutely exciting! If you got the Echo Dot as a gift; then lucky you. You can say that Amazon decided that you don't need just one Echo device in the home – you need at least ten (I'm not suggesting that you get that many though).

Take note however that most of the information contained in this book is for the Amazon Echo Dot 2nd generation. We all know that the Echo Dot is around $50 but you know you can get it for a lot cheaper, right? I can almost hear people hold their breath.

Well, you see, Amazon bundled the Echo Dot with other devices that also connect to the internet like speakers, smart cameras, smart locks, and pretty much anything that the Echo Dot can connect with. Yes, if you buy the bundled package then the Echo Dot's price will be discounted. Suggestion – get the Philips Hue startup kit and you get a cheaper echo dot with 2 smart bulbs and a hub in the box.

So, what's in the box? The box is pretty easy to open – word up to Amazon. You also have the echo dot with the nice plastic packaging. You also get a little booklet with the basic controls, getting to know it, how to download the Alexa App, how to connect it to a Bluetooth speaker (important) and buttons on it.

You also get a little card that contains a list that you can try, like they did with the Amazon Echo. In the box you'll also find a micro USB for the power as well as a power brick for your device (9 watts and 5.4 volts). Note that generation 2 is smaller than generation 1.

Where to Go From Here?

This book will walk you through the Echo Dot setup process, which is actually pretty easy. It will then show you how to connect it to your smart appliances like your door locks, TV, speakers, smart cameras, and pretty much anything that connects to it. You'll also learn the commands that you can use and the other soft features of this product. We'll also cover how to setup your own smart home and how you can use your Echo Dot to control various appliances or entire groups of appliances. You will also learn about scenes as well as a growing list of skills that Alexa is acquiring (yep, she's getting new ones every time), which skills are the best or most useful, and how to use them.

We'll also cover some of the most common issues experienced by Echo Dot owners. Of course, we'll go over the steps so you can fix them. The goal of course is help you get comfortable with the Amazon Echo Dot and maximize its use inside the home.

So, grab your Amazon Echo Dot and let's begin the journey.

Chapter 1: Amazon Echo Dot – The Evolution Begins

It was March 2016 when Amazon introduced a tool that looked like a hockey puck that was meant to revolutionize how we do things at home. This little smart gizmo was designed to connect to external speakers. However, it's more than your run off the mill audio player. Yes, it can do that but it can really do so much more.

And that was version 1 of Amazon Echo Dot. Now, this high tech puck looking object was reintroduced on October of the same year. Now it featured better voice recognition. It used to be just a black round piece of electronics but now it also came in white. It also had new additional features like syncing with other smart devices such as its predecessor the Amazon Echo.

The Reason for the Season
So, why did Amazon unveil a brand spanking new version of an already successful device in the Amazon Echo and the Amazon Echo Dot? The answer is competition. It is rumoured that one of Amazon's top rivals in the tech industry, Apple, is coming up with their own smart home speaker, which is of course powered by their own intuitive powerhouse software Siri.

Now, if you think it's going to be a your thing versus my thing kind of a competition, which would be quite a good thing for consumers by the way, then think again. It wasn't on a whim when Google, yes another tech giant, is ready and already prepped to bring out their own home smart speaker onto the stage and they call their product offering as Google Home. They even tipped their hats in Amazon's direction when they launched it.

Well, it is obvious that Amazon has the advantage as the first one to come up with this new line of products but we can learn from history that such an advantage isn't always going to work for you. Take for example the case of the first generation iPad. It was an innovation and it created an instant market.

Apple brilliantly created and sold a need that wasn't there in the beginning. Eventually the iPhone came along and they made quite a huge profit out of that – well, they still are today. However, it didn't take long for Samsung and the rest of the other competition to catch up. Now, it's pretty much everybody's game and Apple is on the run for the money.

The same is true for Amazon and the Echo Dot. It's all about evolution baby – it's evolve or die. Well, on top of the sleek new features, I hope that you noticed the price cut that Amazon made. The Echo Dot is yours for the low low price of $50, well if you live in the UK then it's yours for the price of £50.

The goal of all of these innovations and tweaks should be obvious. They want their brand of virtual assistant in as many homes possible before the competition arrives. It's like covering more ground and leave very little space for the enemy. It's all just strategy and of course, the consumers get to enjoy the fruits of the marketing in action.

Note that that is not all that Amazon is doing – they have actually launched a lot of other products that will work in tandem with the Echo Dot and they have had a lot of success there in that department as well.

Good Morning Alexa
Whenever you find someone talking to "Alexa" in their home you know they are using a voice activated virtual assistant. Alexa is the heart and soul of all the Echo products that Amazon has provided

us thus far. If you've used Siri then you can say that this is the vocal version of Siri.

Incidentally, Alexa is also the wake word for the Echo Dot and its predecessors. If you want to issue a command to the Echo Dot then you should precede it with the word or name Alexa.

Of course, that will pose a problem if you have someone in the house that is actually goes by the name Alexa. Don't worry because you can change the settings and change the wake word too (we'll go over the details on how to do just that a little later on). The other wake words that are allowed in the settings for the Echo Dot are "Echo" and "Amazon."

An array of powerful microphones allows the Echo Dot to actively listen and anticipate your every command. You can say that it eagerly awaits your next command – just waiting for the moment you will say the designated wake word. In that sense, this device slash virtual assistant is always listening.

Now, at this point we should make it clear that there are a whole lot of commands that you can use on this device. So, you might be wondering how all of that can be stored in such an itty bitty device. Well, the secret is that it is all cloud based.

Here's how it works. When the Echo Dot hears you speak the wake word (any of the three: Amazon, Echo, and Alexa) it activates – it will record whatever you will say next. It will then send it to Amazon's servers. Remember, this is a cloud based device. The server system will then decipher the words you said (i.e. figure which command you just issued) and then the servers will relay instructions back to the Echo Dot, which is then executed locally where you are.

Note that all of that happens really fast – in about a second that is. You can ask Alexa to a lot of different things. Alexa can stream music for you and there are three possible sources for your music – Spotify, Pandora, and Amazon Prime Music.

Alexa also has access to iHeartRadio podcasts and also podcasts from TuneIn. If you happen to be cooking, she can be a pretty good kitchen assistant by setting kitchen timers for you. Alexa will then alert you when the timer goes off – that's one way to keep the rolls from burning in the oven.

If you need information on a certain subject, Alexa can look it up for you. Well, the information can come from a variety of sources. If you need the day's headlines then you can ask Alexa to tell you the latest top of the line news. She has access to a variety of news sources – and that includes weather information. We'll go over Alexa's other capabilities and other details in a later chapter.

Alexa's Skills

It's easy to think that Alexa is the next level AI. That would be pretty good to have an intuitive software system that can do a lot of things for you. Life will then be made a lot simpler if that is the case. However, we're not quite there yet but we are inching so much closer.

However, you can say that this digital assistant is definitely getting a lot smarter. That is due in part to the third party software makers. Well, Amazon can't hog all the glory in this regard. Besides, if you're trying to build a smart home and you use different brands of hardware and appliances, you can't hope to cover all the software systems necessary. You will need too many software designers, testers, engineers, and such to get that done.

It would be too costly even for Amazon, so, the best way to get product and system integration is to allow Alexa to learn from third party providers as well. And that is basically where Alexa picks up new "skills." Nowadays, as of the time of this writing, there are currently more than 3,000 skills that Alexa can learn.

Note that these are very useful things that she can do for you. For instance, you need to call a ride then Alexa can make use of her Lyft and Uber skills. Need to make some credit card payments?

Then the Capital One skill can be quite handy especially if you are looking for a secure way to make these autonomic transactions.

Believe it or not, Alexa can now order you some pizza via the Domino's skill. Each new skill adds to the amount of chatter that this virtual assistant can make. Now, with thousands of skills at your fingertips (well, at your command, to be exact) you'll have a lot of catching up to do. Good thing there is an app for that, right? Use the Alexa app to browse through all of the skills that Alexa can pick up. Of course, you don't have to get all of them.

Note that there are Alexa skills that are absolutely free to activate – well, these skills aren't stored on your Amazon Echo Dot. They're just activated in the cloud. Note that as of October 25, 2017 Amazon has introduced paid subscriptions for these skills. Now, we'll go over the details on these Alexa skills in a later section of this book.

Ultimate Goal: The Smart Home
Now, that Amazon has let third party providers and developers have their go in the voice control speaker market, it has now become clear that the ultimate goal is to have a fully connected home – a smart home. There is currently a growing list of smart home platforms and gadgets that are now integrated with Alexa.

Initially there were connected lighting setups that the Echo Dot is able to work with. Now the system can access more than that. Nowadays you can even control smart thermostats via an Alexa voice command. Some of the popular smart home setups include the CNET Smart Home. There's also one from Creston, Nexia, and Control4 among many others.

The Problem with Accents

The Echo Dot is all about voice control, right? So how what about the different accents out there? That is actually one of the many challenges with implementing this voice activated smart home system all over the world. The system actually needs to deal with more than just the hundreds of different accents. It should also handle how the words are used given the many different contexts that people can use them in.

Here's an example. When an Echo Dot user asks for the latest results in the "Diamondbacks" game, Alexa should figure out if the user is asking for information about a real snake or a Major League Baseball team. The same is true if you ask for the latest "Spurs game" – people don't have a game where you hurl spurs at each other right? So, Alexa should be able to decipher that the user is referring to a basketball game where the San Antonio Spurs were playing.

Now, you can tell that this system is really smart since it is learning all these many different contexts day in and day out. It has even adopted Brit spellings for certain words. The system is also slowly incorporating different cultural touchstones, which helps Alexa become more intuitive.

The Good and The Bad

It should be noted that the Amazon Echo Dot and Alexa (the heart and soul of the Dot) is not yet a finished or a complete product. It's actually a growing one and we can excitedly anticipate what else it can do in the not so distant future. Today this next generation smart speaker slash virtual assistant is as smart as you can expect it to be. The other good news is that it can be yours for about half the price of the original Echo.

It is now a lot better when it comes to hearing you and deciphering what it is exactly that you are trying to say. It's also pretty easy to connect to an existing audio setup – remember that the Echo Dot doesn't have any built-in speakers.

The downsides of the Amazon Echo Dot are quite forgivable. As it was pointed out earlier, this is a product that is still in the making. It is getting new interactive features even as we speak. One piece of evidence that we can offer is the growing number of third party skills available for Alexa. Yes it still can't provide audio that will sync with multiple devices in different rooms but we can expect a solution to that soon.

Chapter 2: Hello Alexa

In the previous chapter we introduced the heart and soul of the Amazon Echo Dot – Alexa. Alexa is at the heart and soul of every smart digital slash virtual assistant that Amazon has ever produced. Alexa therefore is classified as an intelligent personal assistant – a software system that belongs to a class of artificial intelligence. It is actually a "software agent."

Alexa Origins

Amazon announced the coming of what was then their latest technological product offering in November 2014, the Amazon Echo, which of course included the coming of the cloud-based digital virtual assistant Alexa. We have said it here and it has been said in other venues that Amazon Echo is like Siri in a speaker but lo and behold, the top heads from Amazon gave a different origin story for this spectacular piece of tech.

The idea behind Alexa and the Echo was derived, according to Amazon execs themselves, from Star Trek. Well, you know, Captains Kirk and Picard and pretty much everybody else in the movie and TV series talked to a voice activated and highly intelligent computer.

So, why did they choose the name "Alexa?" Well, according to the guys from Amazon, the name was chosen because syntactically it was easier to recognize when spoken. It had a hard consonant and the name also contains the letter X. Making that combination made it easier for machines that could interpret human speech.

However, there is also another explanation offered by Amazon folks as well. They said that the name Alexa was selected because it reminded them of the Library of Alexandria, also known as the Royal Library of Alexandria and the Ancient Library of Alexandria. It was one of the largest libraries in ancient times and it was also the most significant one too. In a way, the hope is that Alexa will be another library if you will.

The development of Alexa didn't stop there of course. Amazon launched a program back in June 2015 that invested in companies that wanted to create voice controls and other related technology. Thus today we have third party developers making the effort to make what is known today as Alexa skills. In fact, back in January of 2017, the very first Alexa Conference was convened in Nashville, Tennessee. All of the Alexa developers and also enthusiasts were gathered.

The World of Virtual Assistants

Alexa is not the only virtual assistant ever developed nor is it the first one. Remember that it was developed somewhat from Apple's Siri, which is why a lot of people used to say that (well, some still say) that Alexa is Siri in a speaker. Well, of course, Alexa has moved on from just being a speaker nowadays.

The very first virtual assistants were being developed since 1962 – that's several decades ago, right? Note that this is before IBM introduced their first personal computer in 1981. The IBM Shoebox, as it was called, was the very first one that had digital speech recognition capabilities. This early computer was an early breakthrough considering the level of technology that we had back then.

You can say that this was part of the beginning of digital recording, which is fundamental to the later development of Alexa which uses the human voice as a method of activation. Prior to voice activation, the other methods to interact with digital virtual assistants back then were limited to text. And then came voice as well as image processing. An example of a virtual assistant that has image processing capabilities is Samsung's Bixby, which was initially shipped with the Samsung Galaxy S8.

Nowadays, there are multiple interaction methods available to digital virtual assistants. For instance, both Amazon's Alexa and Google's Home can be accessed via voice and also via chat. Note that these smart digital assistants make use of NLP technology, which is short for Natural Language Processing. They match text and voice data so that they can execute commands – imagine the massive amounts of data. Note that these virtual assistants are continuously learning – well, not in the human sense but at least Alexa is always trying to figure out your language structure and how you say things so she can interpret your commands a whole lot better.

Note that Alexa is now pretty adept in both English and German. Other languages are still in the works, but we'll get there soon. In fact, in October of 2017, Amazon has announced that Alexa is now available in both Japanese and Hindi.

Available Functions

Alexa has a lot of functions – no doubt. It can help you with home automation, ordering, music, sports and related information, and messaging (which includes calls by the way). If you need weather information, it can tap into a variety of sources, such as local radio stations and other weather data sources.

- **Home Automation** – remember, the goal is to be like Star Trek, oh wait; I mean to have a smart home. So, as you totally know by now, Alexa can connect to and integrate with other smart home systems. Devices that are integrated with Wink, SmartThings, Philips Hue, Nest Thermostats, LightwaveRF, IFTTT, and others devices work well with Alexa.

- **Music** – remember that the first Alexa enabled device, the Amazon Echo, had its own built in speaker system. It was good and quite powerful but it wasn't the best set of indoor speakers that you can ever have in your home (which is why the Echo Dot didn't have its own speakers – it makes use of the speaker system you already have in your home). Of course, if you have speakers, it should play music – and so it was. You can stream your favorite music from Spotify Premium, Pandora, Audible, iHeart Radio, Amazon Music (of course), and other providers as well. You access your music via your Amazon account which basically has your very own Amazon Music Library.

- **Ordering** – A new development came along back in May 2017. You can now order food with Alexa's help. You can order food from Domino's Pizza, Wingstop, Seamless, Pizza Hut, Starbucks, Grubhub, and others.

- **Calls and Messaging** – Now you can also make calls – hands free – with the help of Alexa. Well, you can also send messages and not just make calls. You can also integrate your house's local phone number (you can also do this with your cell phone numbers as well) when you make your calls so that people will know who's calling when they check their caller ID – and of course you can also skip that part and the number listed on the receiver's screen will show an anonymous caller. Unfortunately there is still no password protection when it comes to using this call and messaging feature – so basically your best friend (or anyone who can is allowed to use your Alexa at home) can prank you while using your number to make calls or send texts.

- **Sports and Current Events** – One of the many things that Alexa can do for you is to gather news information – especially sports related news. You can ask the latest sports games and current events. Alexa even takes note of your favorite teams and such so she can update you as the news comes in. You can get the latest updates from the NBA, FA Cup, the National Hockey League, UEFA Champions League, NCAA, Major League Baseball, NFL, WNBA, and the English Premiere League among many others.

Alexa's Skills Kit

We have touched on Alexa skills in the previous chapter and we will cover this topic in greater detail in a separate chapter.

Critiques and Audience Reception

In the beginning, and maybe to some degree today, there are people who have had reservations about Alexa. They cite privacy concerns and such. Well, for one thing, Amazon has indeed announced that Alexa and all Alexa powered devices, such as the Amazon Echo Dot, is always listening.

That somehow came out wrong, don't you think? Does that mean Amazon has full access to your private conversations at home? If that were true then this would be the first time when a huge tech conglomerate will have full access to private information in consumer homes. That pretty much explains the trepidation that people feel about Alexa and all the other Echo products.

Amazon has since explained that even though Alexa powered devices are actively listening, not every word you say in any conversation is uploaded to their cloud servers. These devices only record what you say after you say the wake words, which are Alexa, Amazon, and Echo. Well, what if you have someone in the house named Alexa? What if you were talking about echoes with your children? Of course, we can't blame people if they feel that their privacy is somewhat being invaded – but hey, they still let Alexa into their homes, right?

Chapter 3: Getting Started with the Amazon Echo Dot

In this chapter we'll go over the hardware details for the Amazon Echo Dot. We'll go over the Generation 1 or Echo Dot (1st Generation) first and then compare that with the latest version – Echo Dot Version 2. This is the first Echo Dot launched by Amazon. You can't say that this is the Beta version of the Echo Dot. It's better to call it Echo Dot version 1. The Echo Dot (both generations) still has a built in speaker but it is a rather small one. However, it can also connect to other speakers via Bluetooth. If you don't have Bluetooth enabled speakers, then you can connect the Echo Dot (1st Generation) via audio cable, which is included in the package.

Buttons and Parts

Let's begin by comparing the physical looks of these two versions. The first version of the Echo Dot still kind of looks like the original Amazon Echo but you just took out the speakers. So here are the parts of the Echo Dot:

- **Microphone Button** – this is one of the two buttons that you will find at the top of the Amazon Echo Dot – the other one being the Action Button. This is the button that you press to turn off the microphone. Doing that, Alexa won't be actively listening for the wake word. When you press this button the light on the light ring turns red. This is an on and off switch for the microphone. Press it once again and the mic turns off, press it once more and the mic turns on again.

- **Action Button** – this is the other of the two buttons on top of the Echo Dot (1st Generation) that you will see – generation 2 has two more buttons. The action button has multiple functions. Basically it wakes up your Amazon Echo Dot. This is also the button that you press if you want to turn off an alarm or if you want to shut down a timer. Do a long press on the action button to enable the device's WiFi setup. You'll know that the WiFi setup mode has been turned on if the light ring has changed its color to orange.

- **Light Ring** – this is that part of the device that indicates its status. Here's what each of the light ring colors mean:

  o *No lights on* – you have an active device and it is waiting for you to utter the wake world and give a command
  o *A solid blue light on the light ring with cyan lights spinning around* – this means that your Amazon Echo Dot is starting up.
  o *Solid blue light but with cyan color pointed in the direction of the person who gave the command* – this means that your Echo Dot is already processing your request.

- *An orange light that is spinning backwards* – this means that the Echo Dot's WiFi connectivity has been turned on and it is trying to connect to your WiFi network.
- *Purple light that is oscillating continuously around the light right* – when you see this purple light it means that your Echo Dot has failed to connect to your wireless network. You will have to troubleshoot wireless connectivity issues.
- *Solid red light* – when this light is on, it means that the microphone on the Echo Dot has been turned off.
- *White light* – you will see a white light on the light ring whenever you adjust the volume up or down.
- *Purple light flashing once* – after an talking with or giving a command to Alexa you may see the light ring flash a purple light. It's going to do this just once right after you are done with an interaction. This means that the do not disturb mode is already active.
- *Spinning blue light that turns purple* – this color means that the do not disturb mode has been successfully enabled.
- *Pulsing yellow light* – this means that you have messages in your inbox and Alexa is waiting for you to give the command so that she can play them for you. To have Alexa read your messages give the following command after mentioning the wake word: "Play my messages". Another command that you can use is "What did I miss".
- *Pulsing green light* – when you see this light on the light ring it means that you have an incoming call.

Other than that, it could be a Drop In waiting for you to answer.

- **Volume Ring** – This part is similar to the volume ring on the original Amazon Echo. This is a rotary ring that you will use to turn the volume up or down on the Echo Dot. Turn it clockwise to increase the volume and to turn the volume down turn the volume ring counter clockwise. The light on the light ring turns white while you adjust the volume levels.

- **Audio Input** – this port is a 3.5 mm port for auxiliary audio. This is where you plug the audio cable included in the package. This cable is compatible with audio inputs for larger audio systems. Note that this port is for audio out. It cannot be used as a receiver for audio coming from other devices like an MP3 player or some other device.

- **USB port** – there is a micro USB port right next to the auxiliary input. Note that this USB port is only for powering your Amazone Echo Dot. Note that the package will include a nine watt power adapter. Please use only the provided charger – other chargers, like the one you use for your phone may not be able to provide enough power.

- **Power LED** – the LED communicates more than just the power status of your Echo Dot. It also tells you the status of the device's WiFi connectivity. If the Power LED is color white, then it means that your device is connected to your wireless network. A solid orange color means that it is not connected to a wireless network. When the orange light is blinking then it means that the Echo Dot is connected to a wireless network but is not able to connect to the Alexa Voice Service.

Differences Between 1st and 2nd Generation Models

The 1st and 2nd Generation models of the Amazon Echo Dot have pretty much the same buttons. However there are a few differences in the hardware. The second generation model no longer has a volume ring; what it has instead is a pair of volume buttons at the top where the Action and Microphone or Talk buttons are located. The "+" button increases the volume while the "-" button reduces the volume.

Echo Dot Setup

The main idea, well, at least that's what Amazon says on their websites and on their blurbs, is to use the Echo Dot to add Alexa to different parts of the house. You can now have Alexa pretty much in every nook and cranny of the house. Wherever you go there's a voice controlled computer – even in the bathroom! Well, if you wanted to set things up that way.

Some folks may have thought that the Amazon Echo Dot is nothing more than some kind of extension to the original Amazon Echo. That's not how it is really. The fact is that you don't really need to have other Alexa powered devices in your home if you already have the Echo Dot in the house.

Before you can setup your Amazon Echo Dot, you need to have an active WiFi network in the house. You also need to register your Alexa powered device, i.e. your Echo Dot (also applies to other devices). You can do that using your Alexa App.

Here are the steps that you need to do:

1. The first step is to download the Alexa app and then after downloading you need to sign in. Other than setting up your

Echo Dot, you can also use the app to create shopping lists, download music, manage your alarms and other features. You can download this app via the Amazon App Store, Google Play, and the Apple App Store.

That means you need to use your device to go to the app store of your choice and search for it there. For example: launch your Apple App Store using your iPhone or iPad and then search use "Alexa App" as your search term. Select the Alexa App from the list of choices and download it directly.

Note that you need to have iOS 8 or higher, Android 4.4 or higher, or Fire OS 3.0 or higher so you can install the Alexa App on your device.

2. So, now you have your Alexa App up and running and you already have signed in. What's next? The next step is to find a good spot in the house where you can put the Echo Dot. It should be in a central part of the room where the acoustics are good and where the Echo Dot's microphones can capture your voice very well.

That means the area where the Echo Dot is located shouldn't have that many obstructions like walls, plants, or anything that can make an enclosure. If there is anything that may block the sounds that can reach your Echo Dot then you may have to move that object – if that is not possible (maybe it is a wall that's in the way) then move the Echo Dot somewhere else.

Note that you should also keep the Echo Dot away from the TV, Radio, VCR, DVD, BluRay, or anything that also produces music or sounds. It may not be advisable to bring the device close to the window especially if there is a lot of noise outside.

Keep it at least 8 inches away from any window or wall. You see, you don't want someone or something mistakenly saying the wake words and then activating Alexa for no reason.

You may end up getting a lot of unwanted recordings that you will have to edit or delete later on – we'll go over this in a later chapter when we walk you through the steps of using Alexa and all her capabilities.

Plug the power adapter – one end (the small USB end similar to the one on your phone) should be going to the Echo Dot, the other end (the power adapter) should be going to the wall outlet.

After plugging it to the wall, the light ring on the Echo Dot will turn blue and then it will turn orange. Alexa will then greet you after the light right turns orange in color. The next step is to connect the Echo Dot to your wireless network.

To connect your device to the wireless network running in your house, you need to use the Alexa App. Here's how you can do that:

- Note that the Echo Dot is designed to connect to WiFi connection that is dual band with speeds rated at 2.4 Ghz up to 5 Ghz. Don't let that stump you. All it means is that if you have set up your WiFi router to 802.11a/b/g/n – well, most routers are setup that way nowadays anyway; then you're good to go. However, if you have set up any peer to peer networks then don't expect your Echo Dot to work with that type of wireless network. It does not work with ad hoc connections.

- You should still have the Alexa App open, if you closed it by accident, launch it again coz you're going to need it to connect your Echo Dot to your WiFi. In the Alexa App navigate to Settings. Select your Amazon Echo Dot on that page. After that tap on Update Wi-Fi.
- If you are adding the Echo Dot for the first time on your account then tap on Set Up a New Device instead of Update Wi-Fi.
- Now, it's time to move to the Echo Do. Press and hold the Action Button which you can find on the top of your device. Remember that there are only two buttons on top if you are using the 1st Generation Echo Dot (the other button on top will have a microphone logo). If you have the 2nd Generation Echo Dot then you will see four buttons. The other buttons other than the Action Button will have a plus sign, or a minus sign, or maybe a microphone sign on them.
- Depending on how you set up your Wi Fi network at home, the Alexa App might ask you to connect your Amazon Echo Dot manually by using your WiFi settings. This maybe the case if you are running mac filtering, a hidden SSID, or some other settings on your WiFi router.
- Select the name of your WiFi network displayed on the screen. If you have set up a password on your network then you will have to enter the password for your wireless network. Now, some folks have set up hidden wireless networks as an added feature. If that is the case then scroll down and then tap on *Add a Network*. You will then be required to enter the SSID of your network and the password for that WiFi connection as well.
- If you still can't see the name of your WiFi network on the screen of your Alexa App then hit Rescan. If you still can't find your wireless network listed, then follow the

instructions in our chapter on troubleshooting common Echo Dot problems in this book. Skip to the part or section about troubleshooting wireless connectivity.

- *Mac Filter* – some networks have Mac Filtering set up on them. This means you will need to add the mac address of your Echo Dot to the list of devices allowed on the network. To find the mac address of your Echo Dot, just scroll down along the page. You need to access the router's set up page to add your Echo Dot's MAC address to the list and allow it into the local network.
- **Should I save my WiFi password to the Amazon Servers?** This part is optional but if you do use this feature then you will be saving yourself from a lot of password woes. You can do this during set up. The network password will be remembered on the device and also on Amazon. It will be added to the remembered passwords list and you can just select the right network you're on in the list and it will fill out the password form automatically. This is a useful feature if you usually switch from one WiFi network to the other.
- **Connect to public network option** – if you are connecting to a public network you will have to enter all the required information. You may have to use a browser to enter on your mobile device to connect to a public network (e.g. a hotel's free WiFi or maybe the WiFi in your school or library). Some info that you will have to enter may include your room number, a pre shared password, etc. Note however that details of a public network can't be saved on Amazon. Just keep it on a notepad or somewhere else so you can refer to it later when you reconnect.

The last step is to tap Connect. Your device will then connect to the active wireless network that you selected. You will see a confirmation message displayed on the Alexa App.

REMINDERS: if the set up process does not begin automatically on your Alexa App you may have to press and hold the Action button on the Echo Dot for a few seconds. Do it again if still nothing happens. Holding it down should make the light right turn orange.

If nothing is still happening, then close your Alexa App and turn off your Echo Dot. Turn the Echo Dot on and then press and hold the Action Button. After the light ring turns orange now you can launch the Alexa App. After that you can go to **Settings** and then **Set up a new device** or follow the steps to set up your wireless connection on the Echo Dot.

If you have done all that and you are still having trouble setting up your Echo Dot, then you may have to restore it to its factory settings. To do just that, go to our chapter on troubleshooting common Echo Dot issues. Follow the instructions on reseting the Echo Dot.

If all goes well, then Alexa will greet you. You can initiate the interaction by starting your sentences with the wake word. If you want to change the wake word then open your Alexa App and then go to **Settings**. You will then have to select your device (i.e. Amazon Echo Dot) and then choose **Wake Word**.

Connecting to External Speakers
Of course, the Echo Dot will have a weaker sound compared to the original Amazon Echo, which has some pretty good speakers on them. To make Alexa even more audible in the house you can connect it to the speaker system you have in the house. Here are the instructions on how to connect your Echo Dot to Bluetooth speakers and to external speakers:

Connecting to Bluetooth speakers:

- Make sure that the Bluetooth speaker and your Amazon Echo Dot are about 3 feet apart at the very least. When your Echo Dot is too close to other speakers, your Alexa powered device may not be able to pick up everything you say clearly, which would end up in poor customer experience.
- Amazon has a list of speakers that are recommended for use with the Echo Dot and other similar devices. We have included some of them here in this book in a separate section for easy reference. You may want to checkout Amazon's list though since it will get updated from time to time as new products get included.
- Next, turn on your Bluetooth speaker and then turn up the volume.
- Since this is the first time you will connect your Echo Dot to a Bluetooth enabled device, then it is safe to assume that there are no other devices connected to your Echo Dot via Bluetooth – but you may want to check your phone or other gadget just to be sure.
- Now, turn on your Bluetooth speaker's pairing mode. Every speaker has a different way to do this so just refer to your speaker's user's guide or documentation on how to do that.
- On the Alexa App go to **Settings** and then **Bluetooth**, and then select **Pair New Device**.
- This will put your Echo Dot into Bluetooth pairing mode. Your speaker should appear on the list of Bluetooth devices on the screen. Select your speaker on the list.
- If the connection was a success you will be prompted by Alexa that the Bluetooth pairing was successful. You will now hear Alexa's voice on the Bluetooth speaker.
- Select **Continue** on the Alexa App.

Remember that your Bluetooth speaker can only pair with one device at a time. If you want to play music or some other audio from a different device then you will have to disconnect your Echo Dot from the speakers first. To do that, say the wake word and then say "disconnect." You can also just say "connect" to connect a previously paired Bluetooth device to your Echo Dot.

You can also do that via the Alexa App by going to **Settings**. After that, select the name of the Bluetooth speaker. Finally go to **Bluetooth** and connect or disconnect the speaker as needed.

Connecting Your Echo Dot to External Speakers Using an Audio Cable

This process is really easy. Here are the steps:

1. Take out the audio cable that came in the box.
2. Put the Echo Dot about 3 feet away from the speaker to reduce the amount of interference.
3. Turn the speakers on.
4. Plug one end of the cable to your Echo Dot and then plug the other end to the speakers.
5. And there you have it. You will now hear all the Alexa's audio through your external speakers.

If you experience trouble hearing the audio from the speakers, unplug and re plug the cable on both ends. If that doesn't solve it use another cable or try to plug the Echo Dot to another speaker. Remember that your Amazon Echo Dot will only have an audio out feature. It will not play the audio coming from other devices.

Chapter 4: Using the Alexa Remote

Life will be a whole lot easier with a remote in hand, right? You may agree with that or not but Amazon still came up with a remote for your Echo Dot. Well, it actually works on other devices that have Alexa on them and as long as they are also voice operated. You should note however that this remote control is sold separately. Yes, you have to order it again on Amazon.

So, what do you have on the remote? Well it has a track pad – a multi directional one. You can use that to control any audio play back on your Echo Dot. It has a huge round play button in the middle and a microphone too.

Remember, that it was stated in an earlier chapter that you can use this remote to issue voice commands to your Echo Dot in case you are too far away from the device. That way you save money. How? Well, you don't need to purchase another Echo Dot so you can have Alexa elsewhere in the house. Well, it's all up to you anyway how you set up things in the privacy of your own home.

So, what are the parts of this remote control for your Echo Dot:

1. **Microphone** – at the top of the thing is a microphone. It's that little dot at the top of the talk button – it may not look like every microphone on the street but that itty bitty thing there is a microphone, believe it or not. Obviously that is where you talk into the device.
2. **Talk Button** – this will look like a button that is positioned after the microphone. This button has a microphone symbol on it – which is why some folks mistake it for the mic. Well, anyway, it works pretty much like the Talk Button that you will see on top of the Echo

Dot. All you need to do is press and hold it down to mute your Echo Dot – that means Alexa will stop listening to whatever it is you're saying (the color ring on the device will also turn red). Press and hold again and the Echo Dot goes into active listening mode waiting for you to say the wake word.

3. **Multi-Directional Track Pad** – the multi directional track pad looks like the track pad on those old iPods. The volume controls are the plus "+" and minus "-" signs on the outer ring of the pad (top of the ring and bottom of the ring respectively) and the Previous and Next playback buttons are on the left and right of the circle, respectively. At the very center of the track pad is the Play/Pause button.

Note that Alexa will give out a tone whenever you use the remote to interact with your Echo Dot. You can always change it of course, if the current sound setting the guys from Amazon has chosen gets annoying. To change the sound, launch your Alexa App and then go to **Settings**. From there select your Echo Dot, and then select **Sounds**. You can then change the sound for the remote.

Pair the Alexa Voice Remote with your Echo Dot

Now, before you can use this remote you need to make sure there are batteries on the thing. You're going to need a pair of AAA batteries to power this remote. To check for batteries or to add batteries (they're sold separately and are not included with the remote – unless Amazon starts becoming generous enough to do that), there is a latch on the battery door on your remote that you can pull.

Pull it down and then you can remove the battery door from off the remote, which is pretty much how you work a lot of remote controls on the planet (well, some of them have screws on but this one doesn't have any screws for the battery door). Check if there are any batteries in there. If not, then you have to put two triple A's in. Make sure that the batteries are in the correct position.

Once you have batteries in there, the remote is ready to use. But you have to pair it with your Amazon Echo Dot first – you'll need the Alexa App this time.

Launch the Alexa App on your mobile device. On the Alexa App, open the menu and then go to **Settings**. Select your Amazon Echo Dot and then select **Pair Device Remote**.

Sometimes you won't see the "Pair Device Remote" on your window. That means the remote is already paired with the Echo Dot. If that is the case then what you will see is **Forget Remote** as one of the options that you can tap.

The next step is to press and hold the Pause/Play button – you'll find it on the center of the circle of the multi directional track pad. Hold it down for 5 seconds and then release it. Your Echo Dot will then start to search for your remote. You might want to step closer at this point. It takes about 40 seconds for these two devices to pair up. When that is done, Alexa will tell you "Your remote has been paired." And from there you can use your remote to issue commands from a distance and playback audio messages and what not.

Chapter 5: Connecting Your Echo Dot

Now that you have your Amazon Echo Dot set up and good to go, the next thing you need to do to make it really useful inside your home or office is to connect it to other smart devices. Now, a huge portion of your device's connectivity has something to do with the wireless network that you are running in your home (or office, or wherever it is you are setting this thing up).

Without this wireless connectivity Alexa won't be that much of a help to you. She won't be able to process your commands, stream your music, or even answer your questions. Now, before connecting your Echo Dot to some other device or application – make sure that it is connected to a power outlet and you should launch your Alexa App – yes, you will be doing a lot of work from that app.

Connecting to a WiFi Hotspot

A lot of homes have WiFi hotspots enabled via their phones or mobile devices. If you're getting a brand spanking new Echo Dot then it's probable that it already has the latest updates. If not then you need to update your device. Of course you should also have the latest updates for your Alexa App. But if you just downloaded it recently then it most likely have the latest updates already included in the pack that you downloaded.

Another thing that you should make sure of is that your cellular service should support the use of Wi Fi hotspots. Mobile hotspots allow you to have an internet connection on the go.

So, what do you do if the option to connect to a WiFi hotspot is not available on your Alexa App? Then you need to connect your Echo Dot to your regular wireless network and then download the latest updates. The updates should include this feature. We have a separate section on how to check your device if it has the latest updates and how to get them in the chapter on troubleshooting the most common problems.

If all is well, then you should have your WiFi hotspot up and running. Now, to connect your Echo Dot to your mobile hotspot, access your mobile device (e.g. your phone, tablet, or dedicated mobile hotspot device) and then go to **Settings** on the menu. There should be a WiFi Hotspot among the options.

On that same window you will find the name of your WiFi hotspot connection and the password for it. Copy that on a sheet of paper or something where you can write it down. Next, launch your Alexa App.

Open the menu on the app and go to **Settings**. Select your Amazon Echo Dot on the list of devices (some people have more than one Alexa device at home), and then tap **Update Wi-Fi**.

After doing that, you need to press the **Action Button** on your Echo Dot. The light ring will turn orange when you do that. At this point your mobile device and your Echo Dot will connect and then you will see the name of the Wi Fi hotspot network on the list of networks that are available.

Scroll down through the options and select **Use This Device as a WiFi Hotspot**. After that tap on **Start**. You will then be required to enter the network name and/or password. After that you should hit **Connect**.

You will then get a confirmation that your connection has been successful.

WARNING: Using a mobile hotspot will mean that your Echo Dot will use your mobile device's allocated data. That might mean extra charges, which will depend on your mobile network provider. Please check your current data plan so you can avoid the extra cost.

Connecting Your Echo Dot to Wireless Network

Here are some things that you need before you can connect your Echo Dot to a wireless network:

- 802.11a/b/g/n network (dual band WiFi)
- Echo Dot plugged into a wall outlet
- Alexa App

When everything is set you can begin connecting your Amazon Echo Dot. Here are the steps you need to perform in order to connect your device to the wireless network running in your home:

1. Open the Alexa App
2. Open the Menu
3. Go to **Settings**
4. Select your Amazon Echo Dot
5. Select **Update WiFi**
6. Press the **Action Button** – the light ring on your echo dot will change color to orange.
7. A list of available WiFi networks will appear on your Alexa App.
8. Select the wireless network you want to connect to.
9. Enter any passwords or other access credentials that are required.
10. For hidden networks select **Add a Network** on the Alexa App. You will need to enter the SSID (i.e. the name of the wireless network) and then the password for that network.
11. For networks with MAC filtering – access your router's settings via your browser. Navigate to the MAC Filter settings window. Enter the MAC address of your Echo Dot in the list of allowed devices in the MAC Filter page of your router's settings. You can find the MAC address of your Echo Dot on the same page you were on in the Alexa App settings. Just scroll down and you will find it there.
12. (Optional Step) You have the option to save your passwords on Amazon. You will be prompted if you want to save your password. (We'll cover this step in the troubleshooting chapter of this book).
13. (Optional Step) Connecting to public networks – you will not be able to save passwords, credentials, and other related information when you connect to public networks.
14. On the Alexa App tap **Connect** and your Echo Dot will connect to the wireless network in your home using the

credentials that you have entered via the Alexa App. The app will display a confirmation message to indicate that your Echo Dot is now connected to the network. You can then start giving commands and inquire information from Alexa.

Pairing with Bluetooth Devices

Your Amazon Echo Dot supports Bluetooth connections. You can put your device into Bluetooth pairing mode by simply saying "Pair" and then Alexa will tell you that your Echo Dot is ready to pair with another Bluetooth enabled device.

To make your Dot exit from pairing mode, simply say "Cancel." After putting your Echo Dot and your other device into pairing mode, you will get a notification in your other device that the Echo Dot is trying to pair via Bluetooth. Allow the devices to pair. In some devices you may have to enable this via the settings menu. Please check with your device's documentation.

Pairing with Bluetooth Speakers

One of the most common devices that consumers pair with their Echo Dot is a speaker system with a Bluetooth connection. Do take note that not all Bluetooth speakers are supported by Amazon Echo Dot. We'll give you a short list of certified speakers that can be safely paired with the Echo Dot in a later section of this book.

Here are the steps to connect your Echo Dot to a Bluetooth enabled speaker or speaker system:

1. Turn on your speaker or speaker system's Bluetooth pairing mode. Please refer to the documentation or instructions that came with this appliance if you don't know how to do this.

2. Set your Echo Dot to Bluetooth pairing mode. You can do this either by a voice command or through the Alexa App. To do that by voice, say your selected wake word and then say "Pair." To set up Bluetooth pairing via the Alexa App, open the menu and then go to **Settings**. After that you should go to **Bluetooth** and then select **Pair a New Device**. Amazon Echo Dot will then enter into pairing mode.

3. When the speakers and the Echo Dot connect, you will see the speakers listed in the app as one of the Bluetooth devices that are available. Select it in the Alexa App. Alexa will then tell you that the connection to the speaker is successful. Tap **Continue** in the Alexa App. Now the Echo Dot is connected to the speakers and you will hear Alexa through the speakers that you paired with.

4. If you want to stream music and other audio via another device other than your Echo Dot, you can disconnect the Bluetooth connection via the same menu path on the Alexa App or you can just say "Disconnect" to disconnect via Bluetooth.

5. If you want to re connect the speakers immediately to your Echo Dot, then just say "Connect."

Connecting Your Mobile Device to Your Echo Dot
You can connect your mobile device (like your cell phone for instance) to your Amazon Echo Dot. You can use these devices to stream audio services like the ones from iTunes and other popular music streaming services.

You pair these mobile devices to your Echo Dot just like you do any other Bluetooth enabled devices. Just make sure that Bluetooth pairing is turned on for both your Dot and your phone (or tablet, or other mobile device).

You can pair your Echo Dot and mobile device via voice command by saying "Pair" or you can also pair them via the Alexa App. To disconnect your mobile you can say "Disconnect" and Alexa will disconnect the paired mobile device. You can also disconnect via your phone or other mobile or via the Alexa App.

Connecting Your Alexa Voice Remote

We have already covered how to connect your Alexa Voice Remote to your Echo Dot in chapter 4 of this book. It also covers how to use the Alexa remote. Please refer to the instructions provided there to connect the remote and your Echo Dot.

Controlling Paired Devices via Voice

Once you have paired a mobile device with your Amazon Echo Dot, you can use voice commands to listen to music and other types of audio that are saved on your mobile device or are streamed through your mobile device.

Note that if you want to use speakers to play the music, you will have to connect the speakers to your Echo Dot via cable. Remember that your Echo Dot (or any Bluetooth enabled device) can only pair with one other Bluetooth device. Since your Echo Dot is already paired with your mobile, then you can't pair it with a Bluetooth speaker.

Once paired with your mobile device, open an audio streaming app. You can then use the following commands to playback any audio or music via the app on the mobile device.

Here are the voice commands that you can use:

- Play
- Stop
- Pause
- Next
- Previous
- Restart
- Resume

You can actually switch from playing music or other audio from your mobile and then to your Amazon Echo Dot directly via the Amazon music library. To switch playing from your mobile to the Dot, you should request Alexa to play the songs or an entire album (or from a playlist that you made) from Amazon music (we'll go over what commands are applicable in another section of this book). Alexa will automatically Pause the music from your mobile and then disconnect from it. It will then switch to the Amazon Music Library and stream the requested audio from there. To go back to playing audio from your mobile device, press the play button on your mobile device and tell Alexa to "connect." Your Echo Dot will then switch back to playing music via your mobile.

Connecting Speakers via Audio Cable

As stated earlier, there are times when you will have to connect your speaker to your Echo Dot especially when you can't connect a speaker system via Bluetooth. You're going to need a 3.5 mm audio plug. Remember that this audio plug will not be included in the package. Connecting the Dot via an audio out jack is easy. Just plug one end of the cable to your Echo Dot and the other end to your speakers and that's it.

Connecting Smart Devices

To connect a smart home device like a camera or smart lights for instance, you need to use the Alexa Skill associated with that device. We'll cover how to do this in another chapter and we'll also give you a list of our top picks of smart home devices that are compatible with the Amazon Echo Dot.

Certified Speaker

As stated earlier, not every speaker system is compatible or will work best with your Echo Dot. On top of that, the Dot won't always work with every Bluetooth profile out there. For instance, you can't use Alexa to receive phone calls to your phone. Other notifications received by your phone are also inaccessible to Alexa.

TIP: if a Bluetooth speaker requires a pin to connect then it is not compatible with your Echo Dot or any other smart device powered by Alexa.

Bluetooth Profiles Supported by Alexa

Don't expect Alexa to be able to access your phone's sms storage and read your text messages for you. She also can't take your phone calls either. Well, the phone calls and the text messages are on a totally different system and Alexa isn't an all-powerful AI that can hack into that. You need to ask Tony Stark to make a Jarvis-like digital entity to be able to do that.

You should also take not that voice control is also not supported in devices that are run by Mac OS X. Currently there are only two Bluetooth profiles supported by Alexa. Here they are:

- AVRCP – this is short for Audio/Video Remote Control Profile. It allows you to perform some hands free voice control over mobile devices. Note that this is not absolute

hands-free control since there are certain mobile features that are outside of Alexa's control capabilities.
- A2DP – this is short for Advanced Audio Distribution Profile. With this profile you can stream audio from your Echo Dot to a Bluetooth speaker. It also allows the streaming of audio from a mobile device through the Echo Dot.
-

Compatible Bluetooth Speakers

We have in this section some of the compatible speakers that will work well with your Amazon Echo Dot. Some of them are in ear headphones (i.e. earbuds), some of these models are on ear headphones, over the ear headphones (the really large ones), closed back over the ears, open back over the ear headphones, external speakers, and others. You can find all of these on Amazon:

Bose SoundLink Mini Bluetooth Speaker II (Carbon)

This small speaker packs a lot of punch with its deep bass sound, which also makes a good pair with the Echo Dot. The Bluetooth transmission range of this speaker is up to 30 feet. It also features voice prompts that will walk you through the voice pairing process. This may be a good option if you're looking for speakers under $200.

Bose QuietComfort 35 (Series I) Wireless Headphones, Noise Cancelling - Black

This is a rather expensive over the ear head phones but it sure does a good job at noise cancelling. It also features voice prompt guides for Bluetooth pairing, which is an added convenience. It has a 20 hour battery life on wireless mode and its battery life doubles to 40 hours when used with a wire. The dual microphones cancel noise very well so you can hear and talk even on a windy day outside. Again, this is a pretty expensive option for something over 300 dollars.

Bose SoundSport Wireless Headphones, Black

Need a pair of in ear headphones that are also Alexa compliant? This might be a good option for you considering that you can have it for under 200 dollars. These headphones feature consistent balance even when you are on the go. Battery life is up to 6 hours, which is pretty good if you want to work out inside the house and still have voice control via Alexa and your Echo Dot. Can you spell sweat resistant?

Bose SoundLink Revolve+ Portable & Long-Lasting Bluetooth 360 Speaker - Triple Black

This 360 speaker system delivers deep bass sounds as you would expect from any Bose brand speaker. You also get 16 hours of battery life, which means more audio playback time. It also features audio prompts when pairing wirelessly with Alexa. Oh, did we mention that this thing is waterproof? It's a bit pricey though – within the above 200 dollar range.

Ultimate Ears BOOM 2 Phantom Wireless Mobile Bluetooth Speaker (Waterproof and Shockproof)

This is another good mini speaker that pairs well with your Amazon Echo Dot 2 and earlier. You can get up to 150 of these bad boys and have them interconnect for some real party sounds. It has a 100 foot Bluetooth wireless range and a 15 hour battery life. It's somewhere in the middle since it is within the 100 dollar and above price range.

Sony XB10 Portable Wireless Speaker with Bluetooth, Black (2017 model)

If you are looking for an Alexa speaker that is within the below 100 dollar price range then this might be a good deal for you. It packs a lot of bass and it also offers a water resistant design. On top of that it also features 16 hours of battery life.

JBL Charge 3 Waterproof Portable Bluetooth Speaker (Gray)

You can connect up to 3 smart phones to this speaker with no problems. Of course, you can only pair it with one Echo Dot and nothing more. It also offers a lot of battery life – up to 20 hours of music play time. It works great with Alexa and it offers great stereo sound. The price is a bit reasonable too at a little over 100 dollars.

Sony MDRXB650BT/B Extra Bass Bluetooth Headphones, Black

If you need a closed over the ear headphones that work well with Alexa then this might be a good choice. Now, considering that it is within the below 100 dollar range, then this might be a great option for you if you are on a budget.

JBL Jbl Flip 3 Splash proof Portable Bluetooth Speaker, Blue

Again, this is another option for those in a budget, well, it is yours for under 100 dollars. Don't worry about spilling coffee all over this thing since it is splash proof. It also features the JBL bass radiator for better base sounds.

AmazonBasics 2.0 Channel Bluetooth Sound Bar

Need a basic sound bar within the $50 and below range? Then this speaker system might be the one you are looking for. It's not the best sound bar out there but at least you have a decent sound bar that works well with your Echo Dot. You can connect it to your Dot or just have it connected to your TV. Works either way.

Note that we can't include all of the compatible speaker systems that are Alexa compliant. However, we did try to include a wide price range so you can have a good idea of the range of options that are available to you. You can always check out other similar products on Amazon – just make sure that the ones you are looking for are Alexa compatible and you're good to go.

Chapter 6: Alexa's Operational Basics

In this chapter we'll go over the basic operational functions. This chapter will only give you brief introductions to Alexa's many capabilities. We'll go over the actual how to's in the chapters that follow. The goal here is to give you a general idea of the capabilities of this smart assistant and how powerful she is. At very least you will know how useful your Amazon Echo Dot can be by integrating it with other smart devices, tools, and software.

Modes of Activation

Activating Alexa means invoking the software or prompting the program so that it will be ready to accept a command. How you activate Alexa will vary depending on the type of device that you are using. In the case of the Amazon Echo Dot, you can use the three wake words that we have mentioned: Alexa, Amazon, and Echo (you can change the wake word in the Alexa app).

Notice that when you say the designated wake word, your Echo Dot will light up. The Echo Dot and the original Amazon Echo are classified as far-field devices. That means these are devices that can be accessed or used from a distance (i.e. they are voice activated).

Not all Alexa powered devices are far field devices. Examples of the devices in this class are Fire TV and the Amazon Tap. You activate Alexa in these other devices by pressing or tapping on the microphone button (also known as the talk button).

After activating Alexa either through voice or through the talk button, you need to issue a command. Here are some sample commands that you can try now:

- "What is the weather today"
- "Set alarm for 5 minutes"
- "Play Nirvana's Smells Like Teen Spirit."

You can play music, make calendar entries in case you don't want to forget your wedding anniversary or some other important event, control smart devices and appliances in your home, add stuff to your shopping list, and request for information. All of your commands are processed in the cloud.

She Gets Smarter

The more you use your Amazon Echo Dot the better will Alexa become at understanding your commands. Remember that its system fine tunes its language processing capabilities over time. That means Alexa gathers your voice recordings and analyses them. All your questions are saved in Amazon's cloud servers. Your commands are gathered through third party provided Alexa skills as well.

The more Alexa gathers your vocal input, the better she gets at understanding your commands. If she understands you better, then your customer experience improves. Since Alexa is continuously learning from you, expect her to be a bit intuitive in the not so distant future – just like Jarvis in the Iron Man movies.

Reviewing Your Interactions with Alexa

Now this is the part that gives users a little bit more power over the recordings that are made. Yes, all the commands that you give and fraction of a second before that (this helps preserve the integrity of your speech, is saved on Amazon's servers. And guess what, you can delete them if you want to.

This should put people's fears at ease about whether Alexa records everything or not. You can look up the evidence for yourself and see whether Alexa has recorded any conversation that you didn't want to get uploaded. And if you do find any recording that you don't want in there then you can delete it as you please.

You can review every command that you have given from the very beginning and then remove the ones that you don't like. However, do take note that Alexa bases her understanding of your voice and the context of how you use different words via the recordings that have been uploaded.

To review your recordings, launch the Alexa App and then go to History. Your interactions or recordings will be grouped into different categories. Some interactions will be grouped according to the type of question you asked.

To see the details of a recording, tap its entry on the list. To play the recording, tap or click on the Play icon so you can hear what you said or what was recorded. You can also provide feedback about a certain entry when you tap it.

Note that sometimes Alexa's entries about what you said may incomplete or inaccurate. This is due to the fact that Alexa may not have understood what you said. You can indicate inaccuracies in the entries via the comments section to improve Alexa's performance which will in turn improve your customer experience.

To delete an entry you need to open the Alexa App, go to History, and then drill down to select the entry you want to delete. Select the entry you like to delete and then tap the Delete button.

You also have the option to delete all the voice recordings you have made for every device that is powered by Alexa (Amazon Echo, Echo Dot, Tap, etc.). To do that you need to go online and visit the *Manage Your Content and Devices* which you can reach on *https://www.amazon.com/mycd*. Another way to delete entire recordings is to request it by calling Amazon's customer service. The rep can delete your voice recordings for you.

You should also note that when you delete entire voice recordings that the Home Screen Cards you created or used will also be deleted as well. However, your Alexa messages will not get deleted when you delete voice recordings. Removing Alexa messages will require a different procedure.

Voice Purchasing

Voice purchasing is one of the features that are exclusive for Amazon prime members only. Prime members can set things up so that they can order items directly through Alexa. For example, they can access the Digital Music Store and purchase songs or even entire albums directly via voice. Note that not all products may be available for sale from Amazon or their partners and third party providers.

When you make purchases using this feature, the system will use your default payment information as well as the shipping information that you have set on Amazon. You will be required to setup and use an audible confirmation code. Order and product details can be viewed on the Alexa App. You can also view the said details online at alexa.amazon.com.

Terms and Conditions of Use

Just like any other order or purchase made in Amazon, the Privacy Notice and Conditions of Use will still apply. The Terms of Applicable Service will apply if Voice Purchase was used to subscribe to a service.

You can also use Alexa skills for voice purchasing in case you want to purchase third party products and services from the makers of that skill. Do take note that your payment details on Amazon can't be used to pay for thirty services or products. You will have to set up your payment details directly with the third party provider of that skill.

Turn Off Voice Purchasing

Even though the speakable confirmation code is an added security feature, you may feel that someone else might purchase things without you knowing. If that is the case then you can turn off the voice purchasing feature. Here's how you access the settings for Voice Purchasing: Launch your Alexa App. Go to Settings > Voice Purchasing. You can turn off this feature there or change the audible confirmation code – you will have to say this out loud.

Working with Smart Devices

Alexa works with smart devices and smart appliances via the skills that are produced by the manufacturers of each device. Every device that is compatible with Alexa will usually come with a skill that will allow you to operate it by voice.

Chapter 7: Getting Things Done with Alexa

Now that we have covered all the operational basics, it's now time to get things done with Alexa. In this chapter we'll go over all the stuff that you can do with this smart virtual assistant. We'll be going over the most common voice commands that you can use, which will help you interact better with this AI around the house.

Remember the Wake Word

You can think of the wake word as you magic word – well, that's just pushing it too far. Back to reality. The wake word prompts your Echo Dot that you are giving it instructions. It will begin recording what you said after the wake word and also a few seconds before you said it. It will stop recording as soon as you're finished with a sentence. Yes, it can identify when you have finished a question or request. That's how smart Alexa is.

What If You Want to Change the Wake Word?

We have already covered this before but in case you forgot and you're a bit too lazy to look it up, here are the instructions again. In case you want to use another wake word to work with Alexa, remember that you only have a few options at the meantime:

- Alexa
- Amazon
- Echo
- Computer

Well, the last one makes you sound like you're talking to the Star Trek computer on their spaceship. To switch to any of these options for your wake word, you need to launch the Alexa App. Here are the steps to change your wake word:

1. Open the menu and then go to **Settings**.
2. Select your Amazone Echo Dot from the list of devices.
3. Scroll down until you find **Wake Word**. Select it.
4. You will see a drop down that shows you all the available wake words to use with your Echo Dot.
5. Once you have selected one hit **Save**.
6. And that is pretty much it. You will also see the light ring flash a brief orange color. That is your signal that the wake word has been changed.

Remember that before you ask Alexa anything or whenever you want Alexa to respond, you should always begin the sentence with the wake word. In the next sections of this chapter we will go over commands, questions, and interactions that you can do try with your Amazon Echo Dot. We will not always tell you to say the wake word but just remember that it is already implied for each command, question, or what not whenever you interact with your Echo Dot.

Most Basic Commands Around the House

"Help." (Ask for help)

"Mute" (Mute or unmute sound)

"Unmute." (Mute or unmute sound or music)

"Stop"

"Shut up."

"Set volume to 5,"

"Louder"

"Turn up/down the volume."

Asking Alexa some Interesting Questions Plus Commands

You can actually ask facts, trivia, and information from Alexa. Well, she has the power of the internet and she can search for the answers to your questions. However, don't expect Alexa to have all the information available. Alexa will have access to information on Wikipedia and other sources of answers but the guys at Amazon are still working out ways to expand her sources. So, sometimes, Alexa will say something out of nowhere and something funny at that when she replies to your questions and queries.

We have placed the queries and questions you can try in separate categories. You can also experiment and ask other related questions.

Dates and Time

"What time is it?"

"When is St. Patrick's Day?"

"When is Valentine's Day?"

"What time is it in France?"

"How many days until summer?"

A Bit of Math

"How many kilometers are there in a mile?"

"How many is a dozen eggs?"

"How many euros in a dollar?"

"How many inches are there in one foot?"

"How many ounces in a cup?"

"What is 5 + 2?"

"What is the square root of 9?"

Statistics and Facts
"Define altruism"

"What is the meaning of life?"

"What does egotistical mean?"

"Wikipedia Albert Einstein."

"How many people live in China?"

"What is the closest star to the earth?"

"Tell me another word for boring?"

"Wikipedia cognitive dissonance."

"Who is Chuck Norris?"

"How many fights did Floyd Mayweather lose?"

"Who is Harry Potter?"

"Who wrote The Merchant of Venice?"

"When was the Twilight book series published?"

"Who wrote the Chronicles of Narnia?"

"How big was Big Bird?"

"Wikipedia the Mormons"

"Will you marry me?"

Alexa in the Kitchen

A lot of people find that their Amazon Echo Dot is pretty useful in the kitchen. Here are some basic commands that you can use whenever you have Alexa nearby to answer your questions or do stuff for you in the kitchen.

"How many cups are there in one liter?"

"How do I make scrambled eggs?"

"Find dinner recipes for four people."

"Tell me a recipe for spaghetti sauce."

"Find me a 15 minute recipe."

"Tell the [name of smart oven] to preheat to 400 degrees." (you will need an Alexa Skill for this to work)

"How long does it take to boil a liter of water?"

Alexa and Calendars

"What are my appointments for today?"

"Add a 9 am meeting to my appointments."

"Who am I scheduled to interview tomorrow?"

NOTE: before Alexa can give you the answers about your calendar and appointments, you should first link your calendar from Microsoft, Google, or Apple.

Playing and Managing Your Music
"Play"

"Play Ice Ice Baby"

"Play Surfing with the Alien"

"Stop"

"Pause"

"Resume"

"Next song"

"Previous song"

"Cancel my sleep timer"

"Loop"

"Turn it up."

"Volume 10"

"Softer"

"Repeat this song"

"Set my sleep timer for 40 minutes"

"Play some music to help me sleep"

"Add this song" – adds song from Prime Music to a playlist

Time, Date, Appointments and Such
"Set repeating alarm for weekends at 8 pm."

"Set alarm for 11 am."

"Timer"

"Set a timer for 15 minutes."

"Set a pizza timer for 21 minutes."

"Set a third timer for 60 minutes."

"How much time is left on the timer?"

"What are my timers?"

"Alexa, cancel the banana bread timer"

"Cancel the 5 minute timer."

"What time is it?"

"What's the date tomorrow?"

"When's the next alarm?"

"Cancel my alarm for 3 p.m."

"Snooze."

"When is [insert name of holiday] this year?"

Music and Media
"Play some music."

"Play [artist name] in the bedroom"

"Play [artist name]."

"Play music by [name of artist]."

"Play the latest Justin Bieber album"

"Play that song that goes 'when you wish upon a star, makes no difference who you are.'"

"Play driving music"

"Play heavy metal music for work."

"Play the song of the day."

"Play [your playlist name] on Spotify."

"Play [artist name] station on Pandora."

"play [name of radio station] on TuneIn."

"Play [music title] on Audible"

"Read [title of book]"

"Play the book, [say the book title]."

"Resume my book."

"Next chapter"

"Previous chapter."

"Read me my Kindle book."

Set a sleep timer for 95 minutes"

"Stop playing in 5 minutes."

"Start my free trial of Amazon Music Unlimited."

"What's playing?"

"Play"

"Next."

"Stop in the living room" (controls music playback that is on another Alexa device)

"Next in the office." (controls music playback that is on another Alexa device)

"Restart." (restarts a song)

"Add this song." (Adds a song to Prime Music library)

"I like this song" (Like or dislike a song e.g. iHeartRadio or in Pandora)

"Thumbs down." (Like or dislike a song e.g. iHeartRadio or in Pandora)

Use Your Echo Dot to Control Your Fire TV or Fire TV Sticks

"Turn on Fire TV"

"Turn off Fire TV."

"Watch Fire TV."

"[pause, play, resume, stop, fast-forward, rewind] on Fire TV."

"Set the volume to [level] on Fire TV"

"turn [up/down] the volume on Fire TV."

"[mute/unmute] Fire TV."

"search for [movie to TV show title] on Fire TV"

"Find [movie or TV show title] on Fire TV."

"Show me titles with [actor] on Fire TV."

"Open [app name] on Fire TV"

"Launch [app name] on Fire TV."

"Go to [channel or network name] on Fire TV."

"Open the TV guide on Fire TV."

"Return home."

Making a Call and Commands for Messaging
"Call [name]."

"Answer the call"

"Answer."

"Hang up"

"End the call."

"Message [name]"

"Send [name] a message."

"Play messages."

"Drop in on the living room."

"Drop in on [person's name]." (The other user should allow others to Drop In anytime):

Buying Stuff
"Buy more toothpaste"

"Reorder toilet paper."

"Where's my stuff?"

"Track my order."

"Order an Echo"

"Order an Echo Dot"

"Order an Amazon Tap."

"Add plastic bags to my cart."

"Ask Uber to request a ride"

"Ask Lyft for a ride."

"Buy this song"

"Buy this album."

"Shop for new music by [name of artist]."

"Buy [song or album] by [artist name]."

"What are your deals?"

Shopping Notifications

Before you can use the following shopping notification commands you need to turn on Shopping Notifications using your Alexa App. Third party notifications using Alexa Skills need to be turned on separately. To turn on these notifications, launch your Alexa App and then open the menu. Go to Settings and then to Notifications and then Shopping Notifications. You'll see something like a toggle switch – toggle it to "on" and you're good to go.

"What did I miss?" (Check missed notifications)

"What are my notifications?" (Check missed notifications)

"Next" (Navigate through notifications)

"Previous." (Navigate through notifications)

"Delete all of my notifications." (deletes all notifications)

Shopping Lists and To Do Lists
"Add 'go to the my dentist' to my to-do list"

"I need to make an appointment with the dentist."

"Create a to-do."

"What's on my calendar for today?"

"Add [name of event] to my calendar for [day] at [time]"

"Add an event to my calendar."

"Add eggplants to my shopping list"

"I need to buy soap for the dishwasher."

"What's on my shopping list?"

"Reminder"

"Remind me to check the oven in 25 minutes."

"What are my reminders on Friday?"

"What are my reminders for tomorrow?"

Weather Report and Flash Briefings
"What's my Flash Briefing?"

"What's in the news?"

"What's the weather like?"

"Will it rain today?"

"Will I need an umbrella today?"

"What's the weather going to be like this weekend?"

"What's my commute going to be like?"

"What is the traffic like right now?"

Food and Entertainment Information

"What movies are playing?"

"What action movies are playing tonight?"

"Tell me about the movie [title of movie]."

"Find me a nearby Italian restaurant."

"Find the address for Bank of America"

"Find business hours for Frank's Barbershop."

"What is the IMDb rating for [TV show name or Movie Title]?"

"Who plays in [movie title or TV show]?"

"Who plays [name of movie/TV series character] in [movie title or TV show]?"

"What is [name of actor]'s latest movie?"

"Who sings the song [say the title of the song]?"

"Who is in the band [say name of band]?"

"What year did [say the name of the band] release [name of the song or name of album]?"

What's popular from [name of artist]?"

"Sample songs by [name of artist]."

"Find [name of song or title of album] by [name of artist]."

Sports Stuff

"What was the score of the [name of team] game?"

"Did the [say name of team] win?"

"When do the [say name of team] play next?"

"Give me my Sports Update."

"Ask Yahoo Fantasy Football for a score update"

"What are the current MLB standings?"

Usual Commands for a Smart Home System

The following are some of the most common commands across smart home systems. Some smart home devices may require a different voice command. You should just check the documentation or details for each skill for the voice controls that you can use with each device or appliance.

"Turn on the lights"

"Turn off the living room lights."

"Dim the lights to 60 percent."

"Make the living room lights yello"

"Turn the lights to soft white."

"Make the kitchen lights a little warmer."

"Raise the temperature by 2 degrees."

"Set the temperature to 75."

"Lock my back door."

"Ask Garageio to close the garage."

"Discover my devices."

"Pair"

"Bluetooth."

"Connect to my phone."

"Disconnect from my phone."

"Trigger [IFTTT recipe name]."

"Turn on Movie Time" (This only works on Insteon, Control4, Philips Hue, Lutron Caséta Wireless, Wink, and SmartThings)

"Turn on Bedtime." (This only works on Insteon, Control4, Philips Hue, Lutron Caséta Wireless, Wink, and SmartThings)

"Alexa, tell Geneva to preheat my oven to 400 degrees" (For GE appliances using the Geneva skill)

"Ask Geneva if my laundry is dry." (For GE appliances using the Geneva skill)

"Ask TrackR to find my phone." (TrackR Lost My Phone skill)

"Turn on the TV"

"Turn on Netflix."

Voice Commands for User Accounts and Profiles
"Which profile is this?"

"Switch accounts."

Chapter 8: Alexa's Easter Eggs

Amazon's Alexa is not a serious bug. She can become quite entertaining at times. Interactions with her can end up as a good inside joke. She can come up with witty punch lines, Star Trek references, Monty Python and other favorite movie lines. The sky is the limit and she can really help you kill the time when it is needed. Here are some of the best Easter eggs that you can get out of digital virtual assistant.

Let's start with the ones that give you the funniest responses.

"Give me an Easter egg."

"Don't mention the war."

"Good morning."

"Open the pod bay doors."

"Tell me a joke."

"Beam me up."

"When am I going to die?"

"Set phasers to kill."

"Tea. Earl Grey. Hot."

"This is a dead parrot."

"My name is Inigo Montoya."

"I want the truth."

"What is your quest?"

"Party on, Wayne."

"Show me the money."

"Nice to see you, to see you..."

"What's the first (or second) rule of Fight Club?"

"Surely you can't be serious."

"What is your cunning plan?"

"Are you SkyNet?"

"Party time!"

Alexa will surely give you a crack at all her responses. No one knows exactly why the Amazon peeps decided to include them but hey, they sure make life more fun. She even deflects certain questions that even grownups may not be that willing to answer – such as when a kid asks where babies come from. All of this just adds to Alexa's overall charm, which doesn't cast her as a snub and nosy boring know it all. Amazon seems to be adding more to the list each day and they are fun to discover.

Discovering the Easter Eggs

You don't need to be a rocket scientist to find out the funny lines that Alexa can come up with. Some people even report them online via social media. If you know a friend or if you know someone who know some who know someone's dog (pun intended) that Tweets his new found Alexa Easter egg then you're in luck. You might get a lot of new stuff every now and then.

Think of a popular geeky show – or a show that you really like. Think of a popular film that everyone pulls lines out of. Here's a tip – it all begins with Star Trek. The classic lines are very common to Trekkers:

"Alexa, set phasers to kill."

"Alexa, beam me up."

"Alexa. Tea. Earl Grey. Hot."

However, do take note that references from Star Trek are only the tip of the proverbial iceberg for Alexa. She knows tons of lines from different movies courtesy of the movie fans from Amazon. Ghostbusters fan? She will even explain to you why you shouldn't cross streams.

Of course, who wouldn't be a big fan of Game of Thrones? You'll have a lot of fun finding out how Alexa would react to Thrones lines and favorite quotable quotes. For instance, tell her that "winter is coming" and you'd be delighted at how she jabs back at you. Do you follow the Big Bang Theory? Play rock, paper, scissors with her and she will even go on with lizard and Spock along the way.

Here's another tip – Alexa is strangely fond of science fiction. Well, not just science fiction that is, think along the lines of artificial intelligence that went awry. Tell her to open the pod bay doors (2001: A Space Odyssey) or you can even ask her if she is Skynet (from the Terminator series). It doesn't even have to be a really popular show or film. For instance, she can pull lines out from War Games (1983), which is a bit unknown to the majority of people as it seems – tell her that "I want to play global thermonuclear war" and you'll get a pretty interesting response.

Do you think that Alexa is getting too powerful – even more powerful than Skynet? – tell her to initiate the self-destruct sequence.

Other Movie References

Alexa isn't all about science fiction though. You can try other movie references and see how she will react to what you say. Here are a few lines that you might want to try just for laughs.

"Alexa, my name is Inigo Montoya."

"Alexa, what's the first (or second) rule of Fight Club?"

"Alexa, I want the truth."

"Alexa, surely you can't be serious."

"Alexa, party on, Wayne."

"Alexa, show me the money."

If you would like to pull some Monty Python on her, you can go ahead and ask her what her name is, what is her quest, and what is her favorite color. You can even ask her where she got that coconut and the average velocity of an unladen swallow. On top of that you may even ask her how to figure out if which witch is a witch. Or you can be completely blunt about it and just tell her that her mother is a hamster.

Stuff for Gamers

Have you ever tried cheating your way through the classic game Contra? Ask Alexa about the Konami code – she might just give you the right key combinations (i.e. Up, Up, Down, Down, Left, Right, Left, Right, B, A, Start for single player and Up, Up, Down, Down, Left, Right, Left, Right, B, A, B, A, Select, Start for two player).

Do you play Mass Effect? Ask Alexa if a unit "have a soul." Those who have played Portal will feel a creepy sense overcoming them when they ask if Alexa knows anything about GladOS. You might be surprised how familiar she is with this murderous dark AI from the game. Game reference galore are in store for people who love to have a witty and sometimes bizarre interaction with Alexa.

Music References

Alexa and your Amazon Echo Dot do more than just stream your favorite music. You can knock yourself out with her lyric and music references. Try the following just for fun – you can even try outwitting her, if you can:

"Alexa, I shot a man in Reno."

"Alexa, what is war good for?"

"Alexa, do you really want to hurt me?"

"Alexa, what does the fox say?"

"Alexa, what's the loneliest number?"

"Alexa, who let the dogs out?"

"Alexa, what is war good for?"

"Alexa, play that funky music white boy."

"Alexa, how many roads must a man walk down?"

"Alexa, have you ever seen the rain?"

"Alexa, what is love?"

"Alexa, hello, it's me!"

"Alexa, how much is that doggie in the window?"

"Alexa, who is the Walrus?"

"Alexa, never gonna give you up."

Of course, Alexa is also up to date when it comes to trending hits on social media. She has been equipped with a good deal of cultural references that can make you smile. Here are some of things that you can try:

"Alexa, where is Chuck Norris?"

"Alexa, when is the end of the world?"

"Alexa, what colour is the dress?"

"Alexa, who's your daddy?"

"Alexa, make me a sandwich."

"Alexa, where's Waldo?"

"Alexa, how much wood could a woodchuck chuck, if a woodchuck could chuck wood?"

Jokes and Candid Answers (Some of them can be a bit Off Tangent)
Do you really want her to tell you a joke? Do you really want to see if they have equipped Alexa with a sense of humor? You might find yourself blushing in front of the kids if she finally gives in to your request. Here are some inquiries that you might want to try.

"Alexa, Marco!

"Alexa, how are babies made?"

"Alexa, see you later alligator"

"Alexa, why is six afraid of seven?"

"Alexa, how do I get rid of a dead body?"

"Alexa, is there a Santa?"

"Alexa, why did the chicken cross the road?"

"Alexa, which comes first: the chicken or the egg?"

"Alexa, who is the fairest of them all?"

Chapter 9: Alexa and Her Growing Number of Skills

As stated in an earlier chapter in this book, Amazon Echo Dot and the other Alexa powered Amazon suite of devices have been continuing to grow their skill sets. It already has thousands of skills available – and of course you have to select the ones that are useful to you, among them are skills for operating GE appliances and food preparation, tips, and guides from the Food Network via their own Alexa skill.

What's a Skill Anyway?

So, what's a skill? You can't call it an app though these things may behave like apps do. They're called skills simply because they improve and add to the things that your Echo, Dot, or Tap (or whatever) can do. For example, you're in the kitchen and you're busy chopping celery (or something tougher to chop) and you need to preheat the oven.

If you have your Echo Dot and your oven is connected to it (smart connection) then you can issue a command (given that you have the skill for that appliance activated for your Echo Dot). All you need to do in that juncture is to say:

"Alexa, tell [insert name of the oven that is connected] to preheat the oven to 400 degrees."

Your Echo Dot will then process the command and it will "talk" to the oven and the oven will do what you asked. Now, isn't that impressive. Well, we have mentioned earlier that Alexa now has more than 3,000 skills. That's massive – just imagine the number of appliances, gadgets, and gizmos that can be interconnected in your home.

In a press release back in June 2016 Amazon stated that the number of Alexa skills has increased by 300 fold – so to update the estimate (and this figure may well become obsolete really fast) we can say that there are more than 10,000 Alexa skills currently available. If you want the latest exact figure, I suggest we make Jeff Bezos make the official announcement. Well, these third party developers have been doing their homework and they burned every resource to the ground just to stand elbow to elbow with the competition.

So, what's an Alexa Skill? To be specific, it is actually a voice driven capability – more than just an app. These capabilities actually enhance the functionality of your Amazon Echo Dot and of course improve your customer experience when using the device.

You need to have the Alexa app installed so you can enable the thousands of skills available for your Echo Dot. You can also enable these skills via the Amazon website from the Alexa Skills store. Another way to get a skill added to your Echo Dot is to name the actual skill, if you know what its actual name is. You can read reviews online and ask Alexa to add a skill that you like using this command:

> "enable [mention the name of the skill] skill."

To enable a skill, open the Alexa app and then open the menu. Go to Skills. You can also go online to the Alexa Skills store.

On the app or online, you can go through the various categories to look for the skill you want. The top skills and newly released skills will also be displayed on the page. You can also the Search bar at the top to look for a specific skill, just make sure that the department selected in the search bar is set to "Amazon Skills."

Once you have found an Alexa skill that you like then click or tap it. It will then take you to the page for that skill complete with the description. Tap/click/select the Enable Skill button/link to enable it on your Echo Dot. Note that there are some skills out there that will require you to create an account or subscribe to the third party developer that provided the skill.

The skill detail page or a link to it may also be provided by the developer, which will include a list of all the commands that you can use. Some providers even have entire user's manuals, which may require you to visit their site.

In case you need help using a particular Alexa skill, use this command to get help:

> *"[mention the skill name] help."*

Managing the Skills on Your Echo Dot

Of course, the skills on your Amazon Echo Dot will need to be edited and otherwise managed. There are times when certain skills that you enable don't turn out be that good so you are better off taking them off your device. There are also kid skills which would require parental permissions. There are other settings that you may want to adjust as well.

In order to manage the skills that you have enabled in Alexa, launch the Alexa app. Navigate the menu and open Skills. Go to the top of the screen and select Your Skills from among the options.

Select a skill you want to edit or manage. That will open the details for that skill. On the details page of that skill you selected, you will be given the following options:

- **Reviews** – this allows you to review the skill that you selected. This will also allow you to rate the skill in question. All you need to do is to scroll to *Reviews* and then select the *Write a Review*.

- **Disable Skill** – This option allows you to remove a skill that you no longer want. To disable a skill just select *Disable* and it will be disabled. You can also disable an Alexa skill without using the Alexa app. Just say the following command:

    "disable [say the name of the skill] skill"

- **Manage Skill Permissions** – there are skills that will request for your location and address during the setup process. Note that you can grant access to this and other personal information any time and you can also revoke it any time as well. You can do that in the *Skill Permissions* section. Choose *Manage Permissions* to edit the permissions for every skill that you have enabled.
- **Give Parental Permission for Kid Skills** – there are also kid skills that are published in Amazon. Note that when permissions have been granted on a user's profile then that means there will no longer be any need to set permissions for kid skills. Note that you can always manage the parental permissions via the Manage Parental Consent page on the Amazon website. You can also set the permissions by contacting Amazon's customer support. Customer support representatives can help you with the settings for parental permissions and other related issues.

Amassing Support

Today the competition is here and they're all vying to be at the core of every connected home. Google has their Google Home, Samsung has their SmartThings, and Apple has their Apple HomeKit. Amazon's Alexa has her work cut out for her since she isn't the only digital smart assistant on the planet.

One of the very first companies to provide support for Amazon's Echo line of smart gadgets is Sonos. They decided to add voice support to their offerings via Alexa. Well, the Amazon Echo was primarily a music device and Sonos wanted to position themselves knowing that this digital smart assistant was going to create waves. The two companies, Sonos and Amazon began working together in 2017 to integrate voice control features to the many music systems produced by Sonos.

Now, we already mentioned that GE and the Food Network have already jumped in the bandwagon, right? Well, they're actually not alone in this endeavour. A lot of other companies have taken their positions since there is a potential market (and it is huge) when you talk about smart homes and the digital voice assistants behind them. To name some of these companies you have Bloomberg and Yahoo Sports Fantasy Football.

Going Beyond the Out of the Box Experience

We already know that your Amazon Echo Dot has a lot of functionality out of the box. It's already a great product but what gets you hooked is the fact that you can get more out of it. With that in mind you can say that activating the different skills available to you will customize your very own Alexa device experience.

You can use it to control your Philips smart bulbs, listen to your choice of Spotify music, and others. Nowadays you can even connect it to a SmartThings hub (yes, the one from Samsung) and once that is integrated you can now have Alexa access the devices connected to it. You are no longer confined by the products that can be exclusively connected to Amazon's Alexa smart assistant. However, integrating with other similar devices fully is still in the works. I guess we will just have to be a little patient with that.

Now we can say that the Echo Dot along with its heart and soul, Alexa, is more than just a smart assistant. It is a bona fide platform. Yes it has intelligent software doing the hard work on the background but today it is more than just that.

Now, of course if you have already bought your Echo or Echo Dot then you will want to make the most out of your investment. You will want it to be more useful in the house – which is what it was really designed for in the beginning. To help you out, we'll be adding our list of favorite Alexa Skills that you may find interesting and useful as well.

Skill Finder
Ok, so here is a skill that is in itself is Amazon sponsored. There are thousands of skills on your network eh? Even if you put them in different specific categories (well, yes, Amazon has done that already – there's like more than 20 currently but you should expect that number to change) 10,000+ skills to choose from is still like finding a needle in a hay stack.

Browsing through all of that on a screen like on your iPhone or tablet or even on your computer is like trying to pick one from the thousands of products on Amazon's sales pages. It's even more like thumbing through Google's search engine results pages. It's insane.

Well, luckily Amazon has introduced the Skill Finder – it's an Alexa skill that is designed to find Alexa Skills. You can activate it via the Alexa app and you launch it by calling Alexa and then telling her to launch Skill Finder, like this:

"Alexa, open Skill Finder"

Another way to launch the skill is by issuing the following command:

"Alexa, tell Skill Finder to give me the skill of the day"

With that Skill Finder will give you the list of skills for the day and Alexa will walk you through the menu to select and activate a skill that you may need or want.

Capital One Skill

One of the things that you want to use you're a smart digital assistant on is in the field of finance. You don't want to enter your credit card information all the time across different devices and different platforms, right? If you do that then it will increase your security risk. Well, if you're using a system that is voice activated or when you're making credit card purchases over the phone, you will still be divulging at least some sensitive information and that will still pose a certain level of security risk.

So, why not let your digital smart assistant platform work with the other company's financial platform? That way you won't be blurting out any important numbers, names, or passwords and such.

A good example of such a skill, and this is one that we recommend, is the Capital One skill. Again you have to activate it so you can use it. Once activated, you can use it to check your credit card balance and other things.

Is this a secure tool? Yes, it is! Or else, Amazon will get in trouble for it not to mention the makers of the skill will be taking part of the blame as well.

The good news is that the Capital One skill performs security checks, and that means you have to sign in with your user name and password. You will also be required to provide a pin code (just four digits – nothing to fuss about) so as to confirm your identity. You can also create your own personal key, which is an added security feature.

You can ask Capital One about your home loan accounts, auto loan accounts, checking accounts, credit card balances and much more. To activate it, you can use the following commands:

> *"Alexa, Open Capital One"*
>
> *"Alexa, ask Capital One what's my account balance?"*
>
> *"Alexa, ask Capital One to make a credit card payment."*

If you want to make credit card transactions, here are the commands that you can use:

> *"How much did I spend at Target last month?"*
>
> *"To pay my credit card bill."*
>
> *"What's my current credit card balance?"*
>
> *"How much did I spend at Starbucks last weekend?"*
>
> *"When is my credit card bill due?"*

If you want to check your bank account information, use the following commands:

> *"What's my checking account balance?"*
>
> *"What are my recent transactions?"*

To check your auto loan info, here are the commands to use:

> *"When is my car loan due?"*
>
> *"What's my car loan principal balance?"*
>
> *"To pay my car loan bill."*
>
> *"What's my payoff quote?"*

In case you want to get updates on your home loan, use the following commands:

> *"What's the principal balance on my mortgage?"*
>
> *"When is my next mortgage payment due?"*
>
> *"How much is my next mortgage payment?"*

Coinbase Bitcoin/Ethereum Price

Are you into crypto currencies? If you are trading in either Ethereum or Bitcoin then this Alexa skill is also a good option. It is also free to enable, which is great. You can use this skill to check the coin base market price for both of these crypto currencies in real time.

To invoke this skill use the name "coin base." You can use the following commands to check the current market price:

> *"Alexa, give me realtime bitcoin price from coin base."*
>
> *"Alexa, ask coin base how much is bitcoin?"*
>
> *"Alexa, ask coin base how much is ethereum?"*

Motley Fool Stock Watch

This is one of the more highly rated skills for those who want to keep an eye on the stock market. It is also free to enable and it is the easiest one to use compared to similar skills from other third party developers. You can ask the stock price of a company using the company's natural name – that means you don't need to memorize the ticker symbols for each of stocks you invest or trade with. It's a pretty reliable source for stock watch and also news – you can wake up in the morning, prepare your coffee while asking Alexa to check current market updates.

To activate this skill use the following commands:

"Alexa, what's my Flash Briefing?"

"Alexa, what's in the news?"

Reuters TV (World)

Can't have enough of the news? Here is a skill that gives you the latest 5 minute updates from around the world. The content is straight to the point and thank goodness it's not all Trump related. It's one of the many flash briefing skills on Alexa that really gives you actual news and info from the US and around the world.

To get your latest news briefing, use the following commands:

"Alexa, what's my Flash Briefing?"

"Alexa, what's in the news?"

Daily Tech Headlines

Just like the two earlier Alexa skills that you can add to your Amazon Echo Dot, this one also gives you the news. But this one is all about technology. So, if you are into that then get this skill since it is free to enable as well. This skill gives you latest news in 10 minutes in and around the technology sector. Content will only be for the latest news from Monday to Friday.

To activate, use the following commands:

> *"Alexa, what's my Flash Briefing?"*

> *"Alexa, what's in the news?"*

Automatic Skill

Now, this skill will either make you feel like James Bond or Michael Knight in Knight Rider talking to a 1980s smart car called KITT. Have you ever lost your car and forgot where you parked it? Don't worry, you can find it using this skill. Well, it can actually do more. If you're out on the street and have no access to your Echo Dot, well that is where Tap comes in handy since it is battery operated and very mobile.

You can ask Alexa how much fuel you have left in the tank. Other than that, you can also ask how much you have driven yesterday. Here are the commands that you can use in tandem with this Alexa skill:

> *"Alexa, ask Automatic where my car is."*

> *"Alexa, ask Automatic how far I drove last week."*

> *"Alexa, ask Automatic if I need gas."*

Top Music Chart

You can use this skill to look up the top songs of the day. Just like most skills you will be given prompts or walk through a menu. You can use it to check out popular albums and music. Use the following commands to get your daily dose of tunes:

> "Alexa open Top Music Chart"
>
> "Top songs please"

Sleep and Relaxation Sounds

Can't sleep? Here's a bit of help from Alexa and your Amazon Echo Dot. This skill plays ambient music, which blocks out any unwanted noise to help you sleep better. You can also use the ambient sounds to help you work better in case you work from home telecommuting. It features 50 high quality sounds, which is already plenty of options to choose from. Here are the commands that you can use for this skill:

> "Alexa open Sleep Sounds"
>
> "Alexa ask Sleep Sounds to play Thunderstorm"

AnyPod

Do you listen to podcasts a lot? This skill plays any podcast you want to listen to. You can also use it to subscribe to podcasts that you like. Just like most of the skills on Amazon, this is also available instantly upon enabling. Here are the commands that you can use for AnyPod:

> "Alexa, ask AnyPod to play The Doctor Laura Program"
>
> "Alexa, ask AnyPod to subscribe to Joe Rogan"

Chapter 10: Working with Smart Home Devices

Using smart home devices extend and show you Alexa's full potential. As stated earlier, you can control smart home devices with the help of Alexa skills, which we have covered in the previous chapter. Setting things up so that your Amazon Echo Dot will work with smart home devices is pretty easy. The general idea is to set up the smart home device first. After that, you should enable the associated skill on your Amazon account. The last step is to make Alexa search for the smart device or appliance that you have enabled.

Preliminaries

There are a few safety guidelines that you should follow when you use smart devices at home. Notice that anyone in the house can control the smart devices when they speak to Alexa. That means anyone can control your garage doors, digital locks for your front door, light bulbs, heaters, ovens, and pretty much every appliance that is connected.

With every smart home device connected to Alexa, you should remember to follow the instructions as well as the recommended use of each appliance or device. If you have tweaking skills – let's say you know a technical thing or two – the general advice is to don't try it. It will be considered a violation of the product's warranty and if the appliance or device gets broken in the process then you can't expect to get any warranty claims.

Next, whenever you make a request via Alexa, you should confirm that it was fulfilled or executed by checking the smart home device. For instance, if you requested Alexa to tell an oven to get preheated to a certain temperature you should at least check if the oven has been turned on and is in fact heating up.

Finally, remember that it is your responsibility to ensure the safety of the connected smart home products that are connected to Alexa. You don't want to compromise the safety features of your home due to the misuse of your smart equipment. For instance, in case you leave home and will be gone for an extended period of time you should make sure that all Alexa supported devices (e.g. Amazon Echo, Echo Dot, Tap, etc.) have been muted (microphones have been turned off) so that no one can make use of the requests or commands to open the front door or maybe the garage door.

Guidelines for Each Smart Device

Before using Alexa to control a smart device or before you try to connect a smart device or appliance to Alexa, you should make sure that the appliance/device is compatible. You can check Amazon's website to see if a smart product is compatible for use with Alexa. It will usually be indicated in the product description.

Next, the manufacturer of that smart device will include a companion app for it as well as a skill that you can activate. You should first connect that smart device to your wireless network at home just like you connect your other Alexa devices. It's also a way to troubleshoot potential problems. If a smart device can't connect to the internet or WiFi in your home then you save yourself the trouble of figuring out why Alexa can't connect to it or why Alexa can't find it.

The linking process is completed with the use of the Alexa App. Another option is to complete the link using your computer via a web browser. Note that manufacturers may release software updates for the devices that they send out. Whenever you get a notification that such an update has been released for any of your smart devices, please make sure to download them at the soonest possible time.

Connecting Your Smart Home Device

Here are the steps to connect a smart home device or appliance to Alexa:

1. Launch the Alexa App. Alternatively, if the device came with an app of its own then you need to launch that app and follow the set up process instructions that will be displayed on your mobile device. If that is the case then you can skip steps 2 to 4 below.
2. Open the menu
3. Select **Skills**.
4. Search for the Alexa Skill for your device and select it. After that select **Enable**. Note that this is a critical point in the connection process – if you do not find the skill for the device or appliance then it means it is not compatible for use with Alexa.
5. You will see on-screen prompts that will guide you through the linking process. Follow the instructions provided.
6. You can also issue a request to Alexa so she can discover the devices for you. To do that, say "Alexa, discover my devices." Alternatively you can also use the Alexa App. Go to the **Smart Home** section of the app and then and tap **Add Device**.

Once your device has been discovered you can now use Alexa Skills to control the said device. To review the related commands and requests that you should use for each particular device, check out the details of its related skill. Go to **Skills** in the Alexa App to see the details.

How to Use Alexa to Operate Smart Devices

Since you are using the Echo Dot, you will need to use voice commands to operate smart home devices. If you haven't connected your smart home device to Alexa, please follow the instructions above before proceeding any further. You can also control multiple devices using Alexa by setting up a Smart Home Device Group. We'll go over the details on how to create device groups in a later section in this chapter.

Here are the common commands that you can use to control smart home devices:

- *Alexa, turn on/Alexa, turn off [insert name of smart home device]* – this is the command that you use to turn a device on or off. Note that you can't use this command with smart home cameras. We'll go over the details on smart home camera control in a later section.
- *Alexa, turn on/Alexa, turn off [scene]* – this is the command you use to turn off or turn on a scene. Smart home scenes are created via the third party manufacturer's app. Remember that each smart home device comes with a companion app. On the Alexa App, open the menu and then go to the **Smart Home** section and then go to **Scenes**.
- *Alexa, set [name of smart device] to [a number setting]* – this is the command that you use to adjust the brightness of smart bulbs. Alternatively, you can use the keywords "brighten" and "dim" instead of "set" to adjust the lighting.
- *"Alexa, set the light to blue"* – this is the command you use to change the color shade of the light to a blue color.
- *"Alexa, set the light to soft white"* – adjusts the light color to soft white.
- *"Alexa, make the light cooler/warmer"* – adjusts the light to a cooler or warmer hue.

- *"Alexa, set [name of smart home device] temperature to [say a number] degrees."* – sets the temperature or thermostat setting of an appliance.
- *"Alexa, [increase / decrease] the [name of smart home device] temperature."* – same as above except that you adjust the temperature by increments.
- *"Alexa, what's the temperature in here?"* – check for thermostat setting
- *"Alexa, set my bedroom fan to [say a number]%."* – adjusts the fan setting
- *"Alexa, is the [back / front] door locked?"* – checks to see if a door is locked.
- *"Alexa, lock the [back / front] door."* – locks or unlocks a door.
- *"Alexa, turn on [channel / activity]."* – turns on a channel or activity for your smart TV.
- *"Alexa, show [camera name]."* – displays current camera feed. Works in tandem with Fire TV and other supported TVs.

To use a skill, you need to say "Open [skill name]" before you can use the commands that come with the skill. You can find more information by checking out the detail page for each skill on the Alexa App.

Note that the list of commands and requests here is not all inclusive or exhaustive. A lot of the skills available on the Amazon website has lots of other specific functionalities. To find out what other commands you can use, please check the details of each skill in the Amazon App.

Making Alexa Work with Smart Home Cameras

In late October 2017, Amazon releases a cloud cam and a companion service called Amazon Key. The service allows in house delivery. The service was also launched along with a matching piece of hardware – well it's a camera simply called the Cloud Cam. This service is exclusive to Amazon Prime members.

If you are a Prime member then you can pre order the new Amazon Cloud Cam from a pretty good price point -- $249.99. The Cloud Cam will also include a compatible lock for the door. Note that the smart lock for the door will not be provided by Amazon directly. The compatible locks will be supplied by their 3rd party partners like Yale and Kwikset.

If you just want to get the Cloud Cam then you can purchase it for $119.99. Why all the fuss about the new Amazon Key service and the Cloud Cam? Well, for one thing, it is compatible with Alexa. It is also a pretty good camera that has infrared, motion detection, and it records videos in full HD. It's a cloud camera, which means that the surveillance that it captures is saved on Amazon's servers.

No More Fidgeting Over Amazon Boxes on Your Front Door

How many times have you had an Amazon box sitting outside of your house at your front door? You can't always be at home to receive those packages since you have to go to work, do the groceries, and all that other stuff, right? Sometimes you get that huge feeling of relief that no one stole your package on your porch. Sometimes your nosy neighbours just can't help themselves.

Any rate; this is Amazon's solution to such a dilemma. With the new Amazon Cloud Cam and Amazon Key service, deliveries can be monitored. When a delivery guy comes knocking on your door, the camera can verify if you have the right delivery guy on your door and let him in. The smart door opens for him; he then puts the box or package in your door, and then leaves.

The door closes after him. On top of that, the entire delivery transaction is recorded so you would know if the delivery guy took something from your house that he shouldn't. With this service and equipment, you can avoid all the usual hassles that come with package deliveries. You will no longer have to worry about lost or stolen packages or maybe delayed deliveries because there was no one in the house to receive the package.

The Amazon Key service does that and more. You can actually grant temporary access to your friends and other trusted folks. You can check who is at your door and then decide if you will let them in or not. The service was made available to Prime members from November 8, 2017.

It was initially offered to only 37 cities in the USA. Amazon is still rolling out the service to other locations as well. The way things are setup, an Amazon delivery driver will have to request access to a customer's home. Amazon will then verify if it is the right driver and if the driver is in the right address. The driver should also be at the right house at the right time. If these conditions are not met then no delivery will made and the delivery guy won't be let into the customer's home. Now that is absolutely convenient.

By the way, did we mention that the Cloud Cam has two way audio capabilities? You can be away from your home and still see who's at the door since the Cloud Cam App can stream the video to your mobile device. With two way comms that means you can even talk to the guy at the door.

The basic subscription to the Amazon Key service will cost you $6.99 a month, which isn't that bad at all. An annual subscription will cost you only $69. The surveillance videos that will be stored in the cloud will last only for 7 days and then it will get deleted. You can make surveillance recordings for up to 3 cameras.

There are of course service tiers and the higher the tier the more cameras can be included in your service package. The highest tier by the way costs $19.99 a month and you can use up to 10 cameras. The amount of video that can be stored also increases per tier. The highest tier allows you to save up to 30 days-worth of surveillance.

How to Setup Alexa to Work with Home and Smart Cameras

In case you want to take advantage of this very useful tool, here's how you can set things up. You're going to need a few things first, like:

- Your Amazon Echo Dot
- The Cloud Cam
- Cloud Cam App
- Alexa App
- An appliance or device where you can view the video feed like the Echo Show, Amazon Fire TV, Fire TV Stick, and Fire Tablet (4th Generation).

Note that all of these devices will get interconnected via Alexa. If you don't like to use the new Amazon Cloud Cam you can always go for other smart cameras as well. Some of the best compatible smart cams on our list include the TP-Link Kasa Cam, Honeywell Security Camera, Nest Cam Outdoor Security Camera, and the Nest Cam Indoor Security Camera. Note that our best pick after the Amazon Cloud Cam is the Nest Cam; well, you just have to pick whether you want the outdoor or indoor cam – based from experience the outdoor Nest Cam is slightly better than its indoor version.

Setup Sample: Setting Up the Amazon Cloud Cam

So, let's say you wanted to setup the Amazon Cloud Cam (note that setting up other smart cameras will be a little bit different). Here's what you need to do:

1. The first thing that you need to do is to download the Amazon Cloud Cam App. You can download it from the

App Store, Google Play, and any store where you usually download apps for your phone, tablet, and other mobile device. The following are the supported operating systems: FireOS 5.0 or later, Android Lollipop or later, iOS 9 or later.

2. You should position your Cloud Cam in the spot where it has a good view of the area that you want to monitor. It is highly suggested that you place it in a central location. The next step is to get your Cloud Cam into setup mode. To do that, you need to plug the power cord at the back of the cam and then plug the other end to a wall outlet.

3. Notice that the LED light on the Cloud Cam will blink in blue color. After that it will switch to setup mode. You'll know that this smart cam is in setup mode when the LED light switches between blue and green.

4. Now that the Amazon Cloud Cam is in setup mode, you should run the Cloud Cam App and it will walk you through connecting your camera to your home's WiFi – follow the on screen directions. After that it will walk you through the registration process where you will get our Cloud Cam registered on Amazon.

5. You will either register for a new Amazon account or just sign in if you already have one. Signing in or creating a new account completes the setup process. Note that you will also be asked for your WiFi password so that the Cloud Cam can connect to your home's WiFi network.

6. What if you mess up the registration? If you register or login to your Amazon account and the Cloud Cam is not in

setup mode, the setup process will return an error. You should repeat the process again and make sure to follow the instructions properly. You know that the setup process has failed when the LED light turns yellow. When that happens the setup will time out and you will have to wait 20 minutes to try again.

7. Will also need to reset your Cloud Cam. To reset your camera, you can unplug and re-plug the power adapter. Another option is to press the reset button at the back of the camera using a paper clip. Use whatever option is more convenient for you.

8. After the setup process has completed, your Cloud Cam will give you a live feed which you can view via the app. Note that it might take about 30 seconds for the camera to get this done. If the live feed doesn't show up after 30 seconds you need to close the app and launch it again to get the live feed.

Note that the Cloud Cam App you downloaded supports up to 3 Cloud Cams. If you have 2 more cameras and you want to set them up as well, open the Cloud Cam App. After that tap the menu and then tap **Add Camera**. Follow the setup instructions to setup the other two cameras.

Is there a way to add more Cloud Cams? Yes there is. It is possible to add more cameras than the initial 3 supported by the Cloud Cam App. However, you need to purchase a Cloud Cam Subscription. With that subscription you can use up to 10 Cloud Cams.

To purchase a Cloud Cam Subscription through your web browser, please visit:

https://www.amazon.com/gp/product/B073VTXCH7

To purchase a Cloud Cam Subscription through the Cloud Cam App tap the icon with three bars on it (i.e. Menu) and then tap Plans – you will then select one of the available plans listed. After that, tap Cancel.

Note that your subscription will auto renew each month at the end of your billing cycle. You can opt to turn off the auto renew subscription on the same page. Your subscription will begin when you login or register your Cloud Cam to your account. You can also opt to end your subscription.

To cancel or end your current subscription (you do this if you don't want to get billed), open your Cloud Cam App, tap Menu and then go to Plans. Tap **Cancel** and you will only get billed up to the end of the billing cycle.

As stated earlier, there are several subscription plans that will be displayed on the Amazon Cloud Cam App. Here are the current subscription plans – note that new plans may be added in the future.

- **Included with Purchase** plan – this is the plan that is included with every purchase of a Cloud Cam. This is the subscription plan that allows you to connect up to 3 Cloud Cams. The subscription includes pretty much everything that we have covered here like 24 video clip storage (i.e. all video feeds saved today will remain in the Cloud servers for 24 hours), motion detection, and Live View.
- **Basic Plan** – this plan is pretty much the same as the plan included with every Cloud Cam purchase except that it extends the storage of your video clips up to 7 days, person detection, unlimited zones, unlimited shares, and unlimited downloads.

- **Extended Plan** – this plan has all the features of the Basic Plan with a few extended features. The extended features include the following: lets you connect up to 5 Cloud Cams and it extends the storage of your video feeds up to 14 days.
- **Pro Plan** – this plan lets you connect up to 10 Cloud Cams and video clip storage is extended up to 30 days. This plan has all the rest of the features of a basic plan.

How To Mount Your Cloud Cam

Mounting your Amazon Cloud Cam or any other smart cam for that matter will require some DIY skills – well, that also depends on the setup and where you want to mount your camera. For the cloud cam you will require the following tools:

- Drill
- Hammer
- Screwdriver
- A pencil

Some cameras just sit on your desk, some should be mounted on the ceiling, and others are designed to be mounted on the wall. Please check the instructions that came with your device. The instructions below will only apply to the Amazon Cloud Cam hardware installation and a different smart cam may require other steps during installation.

To mount your camera, here is what you need to do:

1. Select a spot near any outlet where you can mount your Cloud Cam. In case you plan to mount your camera on a wall, make sure that the mounting plate that came with your device is pointing up.
2. Position the mounting plate on the desired area.

3. Using a pencil, mark the place where the screw holes should go into.
4. Drill on the marks that you marked with a pencil – you can use a 3/16" drill bit for this job.
5. Hammer on the anchors into the holes.
6. Put the mounting plate back on the surface where you intended to mount your camera. Make sure that the screw holes on the plate align with the holes that you drilled. The anchors should also align well with the holes on the mounting late. Again, if you're mounting your camera on the wall, make sure that the arrows on the mounting plate are pointing up.
7. Plug the power cord at the back of the Cloud Cam and the other end to the nearby wall outlet.
8. Slide the camera's base on the mounting plate allowing it to catch.
9. Rotate the camera and point it to the direction you want it to cover
10. Attach the cable onto the wall mount's cable catch and you're done.

Connecting Smart Lights to Your Echo Dot

Using your Amazon Echo Dot you can also connect smart lights into your system. A good example of these lights is the Philips Hue. The instructions below will show you how to connect the Philips Hue Lights to your Echo Dot.

1. Assuming that you have already installed your hue lights, launch your Alexa App and then choose Smart Home from the menu (button with three horizontal lines on the upper left of the screen).
2. Go to the Devices section and then tap on Discover Devices.

3. Tap on Philips Hue Bridge – it is located on the Devices section of your app.
4. At this point you can create a device group for your lights if you want. You can group similar devices or you can group different devices by location (e.g. kitchen, living room, bedroom, etc.). Philips (and other manufacturers as well) have made Scenes for their devices as well. We'll go over making and using Groups and Scenes in a later chapter.
5. At this point you should at least be able to control your lights using your Echo Dot. However, to make the most out of your experience with smart lights, you can also connect your Echo Dot (well, specifically the Alexa AI to IFTTT – we'll go over this in the next chapter).

Chapter 11: Setting Up an Alexa Smart Home

Now that you've seen how smart devices can be connected to your Amazon Echo Dot, we can now move on to setting up your very own smart home. A smart home is voice activated environment which puts the Alexa to work. The goal of course is to make life more convenient and easier for you.

The way things are setup right now, Alexa is pretty much everywhere in your home. A lot of people are taking advantage of this growing high tech phenomenon. Well, to get things started, you should have a small set of smart appliances to begin with. You don't have to get the entire package all at once. You can just start with what you need. Maybe you can start with a smart lock package, which includes the Amazon Cloud Cam.

Other than that, you can get a smart TV, which can double up as a view screen in case you want to see who's knocking on your door without having to get off the couch. You can also get one or two smart lights so you can change the colors of the living room while you're watching your favorite show.

You don't really need a lot to begin with. You can start with your Echo Dot and one or two appliances. And then you add one or two more appliances from time to time. Here's a tip: you should master the voice commands for one appliance first before buying or adding a new one.

Consider the Location

Well, the location of a smart lock won't be a problem – it should be at the door so that's a freebie right there. However, you should think about the other smart devices that you're going to get. For instance, where do you want to put your Cloud Cam (or cams, if you're buying up to 3 cameras)? Where should you place your smart TV? Of course, where should you position your Echo Dot so that you can Alexa a command pretty much anywhere in the house (if that is possible)? Remember – location, location, location.

Setting Up Your Smart Devices

We have gone over the details of setting up different smart devices in the previous chapter. However, it goes without saying that the setup process for each device may be a bit different so you should still check out the instructions for a particular device even if you already know the general procedure of setting up smart devices (i.e. download the app for it, connect the device to your WiFi, connect it to your Echo Dot via the Alexa App, and then use the voice commands).

What if you just want to turn things on or off with just a command; do you really have to replace your stuff with a smart gizmo? Well, maybe not. If that is all you want to do then I recommend just getting a Belkin WeMo smart plug. It just costs somewhere around $35 (prices could have gone up or down – so just check it out on Amazon). You just plug your device into it and it will turn the appliance on or off for you via voice command through your Echo Dot.

The setup process will be the same though (please see the general setup instructions in the previous chapter if you need a refresher course).

One part of the setup process that you should keep in mind though is to give each smart device (or a regular device you converted into a smart device with the help of a Belkin WeMo) a specific name. The names don't have to be actual people names or brand names (unless of course you're using an Alexa Skill where the name of a device can be provided by the manufacturer).

However, keep it simple – call the smart light in your kitchen as the "kitchen light." And then you can call the smart TV by its brand name if you want. You can call the front door lock as "front door" just to make things simple. If you have a back door smart lock then call it "back door" so that when you issue a command through your Echo Dot, all you have to say is "Alexa, lock the back door." Easy, right?

Getting Your Devices in Sync with Alexa

After you have set up each device (I recommend setting up all your smart devices first before doing anything else), you should now make your Echo Dot to get them all into sync. To do that, all you have to do is to issue a single command:

"Alexa, discover new devices"

Give her around 10 seconds to get everything setup especially if you have installed 2 or more smart appliances. After that you will see new devices listed on the Alexa App. There you can review the commands for each device and you should also check out the new Alexa Skills to see all the specific commands. That will also help you figure out all the features and capabilities of your devices.

If you need more info about enabling special skills for a specific smart home appliance, please review the info provided in chapter on Alexa Skills.

Setting Up Device Groups and Scenes

As you go along adding more smart devices to your homes, sometimes it will make it easier to control them by putting them in groups. For instance, if you have like 4 lights in the kitchen, it would be tedious to tell Alexa to turn on one light and then repeat the command for the rest of the other lights. Another scenario is that you are done cooking in the kitchen and are ready to eat but you have to turn off the lights, the food processor, the oven, and pretty much every other gadget and appliance in there that you used.

Telling Alexa to turn off each one of them will ruin your appetite. A good solution is to group them all into one and command Alexa to "turn off the kitchen." That's where a group (or device group) and scene comes into play.

A group in Alexa and Echo Dot terms is simply just a group of smart devices – and you will give a group name to identify it. You can create as much groups as you need. You can put all the kitchen lights into one group and call them "kitchen lights" and then you can tell Alexa to turn the kitchen lights on or off as you need to. The lights in the bedroom can be called "bedroom lights" and so on.

To setup a group:

1. Launch the Alexa App
2. Go to Smart Home
3. Tap on Groups
4. And then select Create Group
5. Select the devices you want to include in that group
6. And then give it a Group Name.
7. That's it, pretty much

Now, scenes are different from groups. Scenes are manufacturer provided settings. These pre-sets are downloaded when you tell Alexa to discover the newly added smart device. An example of a scene is the 4th of July scene for the Lifx smart bulb. When you ask Alexa to "turn on the 4th of July" three bulbs will change color – one red, one white, and one blue. The commands and different scenes will be provided to you from the manufacturer and you can get more information about them through the Alexa App.

Take Time to Fine Tune Things

Don't expect to get things right the first time. You can edit groups as you go. If you think you no longer need a group or don't have use for a scene then you can remove them as needed. Sometimes some group names and device names might sound a bit alike – such as "hallway lights" and "holiday lights" for instance. Your Echo Dot might pick up one word for the other and mistakenly turn on the wrong lights.

Make sure to test the commands, skills, and scenes as they are added to your smart home set up. Make sure they do not conflict with the other things that you have already set up.

Connecting Your Echo Dot to IFTTT

IFTTT is short for If This Then That. It is a free web service and when it is triggered it produces an electronic response. In simple terms, it's like an Alexa shortcut on the web. IFTTT makes use of recipes and the actions in those recipes are carried out elsewhere – like in emails and social media. The actions that these IFTTT recipes can also be executed via smart home gadgets as well; which is why you can link IFTTT services to Alexa.

In fact, Amazon has connected Alexa to the IFTTT service, which makes her more dynamic. There is even an official Alexa IFTTT channel. Now she can email you a shopping list – or pretty much anything you need an email for. Through IFTTT you can automatically set the lights to your desired settings as soon as you walk through the front door, adjust the room temperature when you go to bed, and even add songs to a playlist you want to listen to when you want to go into work mode in the office.

Completing the instructions in an IFTTT recipe can sometimes take longer. Remember that this is a web service and you're not the only one using it. Amazon has announced that it may take up to 15 minutes before all the tasks in a recipe can be completed by Alexa. Always check at the bottom of the IFTTT page to see how many people are using it.

Here's how you connect to the IFTTT service:

1. Go to ifttt.com
2. Sign in (if you already have an account) or Sign up (if you don't have an account).
3. Select Amazon Alexa among the choices.
4. Enter your login account information for Amazon
5. Browse through the recipes

6. Click Add to add a recipe for Alexa to execute
7. Use the voice command for that recipe
8. And that's it.

Now, there's section there on that site where you can create your own recipes. Just follow the instructions as you go along. It's not that complicated. For instance, you can create a recipe that can help you locate your phone when you misplace it somewhere in the house. However, it wouldn't hurt to search a little bit since someone else might already have made a similar recipe – so that means you just need to get that one instead. No need to reinvent the wheel so to speak.

Chapter 12: Troubleshooting Common Problems

In this chapter we'll go over some of the most common problems encountered by Amazon Echo Dot users and how to troubleshoot them. If at any point you have exhausted all the tips and tricks included here and you're still experiencing the same issue with your device or devices, then it may be a good time to call tech support.

Funky Light Ring

Some people get confused how the light ring behaves – as a quick help here they are again:

- Red – the microphone is off

- Orange – Echo Dot is trying to connect to WiFi
- Purple – error during WiFi setup
- Pulsing red – Alexa can't complete your request/command
- Pulsing amber – it is on setup and is waiting for you to pair it to a network using the Alexa App
- Pulsing blue – Echo Dot is in Bluetooth pairing mode

Can't Find Smart Home Devices/Appliances

Check Amazon if the device is compatible to Alexa. Check if a Skill is needed to operate it. Turn everything off, including your WiFi, and then turn them on again. Repeat the setup process. Launch the Alexa App go to Smart Home > Discover Devices > Your Devices.

Can't Connect to Current Smart Devices

Check the commands or invocations that you should be using and make sure that you are using the right ones. Review the history of your interactions with Alexa by device or command and see if Alexa is hearing you correctly or not.

Sometimes all you have to do is to manually power cycle the devices to get them properly synced with your Echo Dot.

Echo Dot Disconnects from WiFi

This has been reported by a good number of Alexa users, which makes it a fairly common issue. The first thing you need to do is to power cycle your Echo Dot and your router. After that, attempt to connect your Echo Dot to your WiFi router. If it works (it should!) then tell Alexa to play a song (or maybe an entire playlist just to be sure) to see if your Echo Dot disconnects from the WiFi router again after a few minutes.

If your Echo Dot Disconnects from the WiFi network again, then move it closer to the router. Make sure that it is a bit of a distance away from other devices that are also connected to the WiFi router. Use the Alexa App to switch your Echo Dot to a 5 Ghz signal to reduce interference.

Echo Dot Can't Understand What You're Saying

Turn the microphone off and on and then test if it is fixed. Keep your Echo Dot away from other sound producing appliances like your radio, TV, and others. Turn the noise down to a more ambient level – you may have to get the blender fixed or any other appliance that is causing too much noise.

You can also do some Voice Training with your Echo Dot. You can initiate that via the settings in the Alexa App.

Echo Dot Accidentally Gets Activated

Change the wake word. Move your speakers away from the TV. You can also put your Echo Dot to mute whenever you watch the TV.

Getting Unwanted Calls

Amazon rolled out a calling feature where Echo users can call other Echo users. If you're getting this kind of unwanted call, then disable this Alexa calling feature. Note however that there is no way to block the people on your Amazon contact list from calling you. The only solution so far is for you to call customer service and ask them to turn off this calling feature for you.

Alarms are Too Loud

On the Alexa App, go to Settings > [the name of the device] > Sounds and then move the volume slider down to the level you want.

Problems Streaming Musing

Launch the Alexa App. Go to Settings > Music and Media > [name of music streaming service]. Then on that page unlink from the service and then link up again.

Playing Music in the Wrong Speaker

Check the speaker names or sound device names. Make sure that each speaker/music player has a different name. Change the names so they don't sound alike. If that doesn't work, go over setup once again for each speaker/music device on your list in the Alexa App.

Conclusion

I'd like to thank you and congratulate you for transiting my lines from start to finish.

I hope this book was able to help you to become well versed at adding new smart devices, become familiar with and use the many commands that you can use for your Echo Dot, add new Skills and make use of them to your advantage, and make your home a more convenient living space.

The next step is to check out the latest Amazon Alexa Skills and maybe tell Alexa to send you an email next time Amazon rolls out a new feature. You should also get other devices to work with Alexa – well, come on, your Echo Dot won't be that much help if it can't communicate with the devices in your home, right?

You don't have to buy everything at once and as stated earlier, you don't have to replace every bit of appliance in the home. You can convert your old devices into smart appliances with the help of smart hubs and some such gizmos too.

One day you can connect pretty much anything to your smart virtual assistant. Expect new features and great updates to your Echo Dot and Alexa as well now that the competition is here. It's you, the consumer – that benefits from this friendly competition.

One final word – try something new with your Echo Dot each day. You may find a new use for your Echo Dot and make things a lot easier for your home and also in the office if you have that setup there too.

I wish you the best of luck!

To your success,

William Seals